Anonymous

Report and Testimony of the Committee on Investigation

In the Case of Hon. Alfred Spates

Anonymous

Report and Testimony of the Committee on Investigation
In the Case of Hon. Alfred Spates

ISBN/EAN: 9783337161613

Printed in Europe, USA, Canada, Australia, Japan

Cover: Foto ©ninafisch / pixelio.de

More available books at **www.hansebooks.com**

TESTIMONY.

REPORT OF THE COMMITTEE ON ACCOUNTS.

The Committee on Accounts, who were directed by a resolution of the Board to examine and report upon the accounts of Alfred Spates, Esq., the late President of the Chesapeake and Ohio Canal Company, beg leave to report:

That they have found the task imposed upon them much more laborious and important than they expected, and, although they have bestowed much time upon it, the meeting of the Board find them unprepared to make a full and final report. The results of their investigations, as far as they have been prosecuted, are however so serious that they do not feel themselves at liberty to postpone communicating them to the Board at its present session.

Soon after the Committtee commenced their labors, they found that it would be necessary to hold a session in the city of Cumberland, and they considered it just to Mr. Spates that he should have an opportunity to be present at their meetings. They accordingly notified him in writing of the time and place of meeting, and afterwards of the particular points to which they then intended to direct their inquiries. He declined to meet them, for reasons which the Board will have full opportunity to appreciate, from his letter, which the Committee communicate with this report. Left to their own guidance, without the advantage of Mr. Spates' explanations, the Committee proceeded with their investigation, and now submit the conclusions to which they arrived and the evidence upon which they are founded.

First.—On the 30th of November, 1867, the late President, Mr. Spates, directed Isaac R. Mans, Superintendent of the Georgetown Division, to send to him $826.00 to pay for an ice breaker and cooking stove and fixtures, which had been built at Cumberland for the use of the Georgetown Division. In his letter requiring this money to be sent to him, he promises Mans that he will pay for the ice breaker and fixtures, get the proper vouchers, and send them to him by mail. On the second of December Mr. Spates writes to Mans acknowledging the receipt of the money, and promising to send receipts to-morrow, and on the third he accordingly sends to Mans a bill and receipt, of which the following is a copy:

CUMBERLAND, MD.
CHESAPEAKE AND OHIO CANAL COMPANY.
1867.   To THOMAS SHERIDAN, DR.
Dec. 3rd. To building, ironing, painting and finishing one Ice
   Breaker for use of Georgetown Division......... $800 00
Received payment of Isaac R. Mans, Sup't Georgetown Division.
                                THOMAS SHERIDAN.

When this receipt was brought to the attention of the Committee, it became apparent to them that the hand-writing and signature were very unlike the writing of Mr. Sheridan, which they found upon other papers in the office of the Company. They therefore called Mr. Sheridan before them, and exhibited to him the paper bearing his name. He at once pronounced it a fabrication, and without hesitation confirmed his declaration in the most solemn manner by the affidavit which the Committee submit with this report.

The ice breaker, which was thus attributed to Mr. Sheridan, had been built by the Superintendent of the Cumberland Division, and paid for by that officer, and the payment allowed to him in his accounts. The bill and receipt purporting to be executed by Mr. Sheridan, was, as the Board will perceive, regularly signed, dated and stamped, and bore all the outward marks of a genuine paper, and Mr. Mans, treating it as such, filed it as a voucher with his statement No. 11. of expenses for November, 1867. The circumstances are such as to show, beyond all reasonable doubt, that this paper was fabricated, or caused to be fabricated, by Mr. Spates. The money which it represented was remitted directly by Mans to him, and the fabricated paper was sent to Mans by Mr. Spates without the intervention of any third person. Its direct effect was to leave in the hands of Mr. Spates the whole sum of eight hundred dollars, and to cause the Company to pay twice for the same ice breaker.

Second.—In the month of October, 1868, John Shay, Superintendent of the Antietam Division, presented an estimate for ordinary expenses, and for work authorized to be done, amounting to $1,465.83. By direction of the President, Mr. Fawcett, the clerk, added to this estimate the sum of one thousand dollars for a scow, lumber and paddle frames. By the affidavit of John Shay, it appears that the President undertook the expenditure of $1,000 dollars of this money, and that he chose Cumberland as the proper place for its disbursement. To enable Mr. Shay to settle his account, he sent him a number of vouchers, amongst which was a bill and receipt of J. J. Bruce, for lumber, dated November 9th, 1868, for $652.60. The affidavit of Mr. Bruce shows that of this bill $400 had been paid by Mr. Sprigg, Superintendent of the Cumberland Division, and of course it results that Mr. Spates gained and the Company lost exactly that sum by the transaction. In this case, like the last, there was no second or third person coming between Mr. Spates and Mr. Shay. The money proceeded directly from Shay to Spates, and the duplicated receipts directly from Spates to Shay.

Third.—In October, 1868, Isaac N. Mans, the Superintendent of the Georgetown Division, presented his estimate for ordinary expenses and for work authorized to be done, amounting to $2,496.79, when Mr. Fawcett, by order of the President, added to it $150 for a scow and transportation, making the whole amount $2,946.79. Of course, this scow was also to be built in Cumberland, and Mr. Spates took upon himself the burthen of disbursing $400 of Mr. Mans' appropriation, and Mr. Mans paid him that amount. In order to enable the latter officer to settle his account, Mr. Spates sent to him the bill and receipt of J. J. Bruce for $400, dated November 9th, 1868, which Mr. Mans filed as his voucher. But Mr. Bruce's affidavit shows that this bill and receipt was a mere duplicate, that no money was paid to him for it by Mr. Spates; that the lumber which it represented had already been paid for by Mr. Sprigg, and, of course, the result to Mr. Spates and to the Company is exactly the same as in the case of Mr. Shay.

Fourth.—In October, 1868, Mr. George W. Spates, Superintendent of the Seneca Division, presented his estimate for ordinary expenses and for work authorized to be done, amounting to the large sum of $3,193.61. Amongst the objects of the expenditures, under the head of " For other purposes," was " one new house boat," and one new scow, $1,225. Mr. George W. Spates drew three thousand one hundred dollars, in payment of this estimate, on the 5th of November, and, according to his own statement, proceeded to Cumberland, and there disbursed so much of it as was necessary for the house boat and scow, and in settlement of his account he filed, as vouchers, two bills and receipts of " H. P. Tasker & Co."; one dated November 9th, 1868, for $1,200, and the other, dated November 18th, 1868, for $150.

Your Committee called Mr. Tasker before them and exhibited to him these bills and receipts. They had all the requisite *prima facie* appearance of being genuine. They were drawn out with great particularity as to dates and amounts; were upon the printed bill-heads used by the firm of H. P. Tasker & Co., and one of them set out that the lumber and material was for an " Ice breaker and a house boat, built for the Seneca Division, by order of the Canal Board." Notwithstanding all these convincing proofs of their genuine character, Mr. Tasker and his clerk pronounced them fabrications, and their affidavit, herewith filed, shows that they never sold the lumber or materials to Mr. George W. Spates or to the Canal Company, or to any one, on behalf of either, and never executed any such bills or receipts at any time. Your Committee felt bound to call Mr. George W. Spates before them and to give him an opportunity to explain. He persists in declaring that the bills were sent to him *unreceipted* from Cumberland by some one, he does not know by whom; that he took them to Cumberland and paid the money, he does not know to whom, nor whether at the counting house of " H. P. Tasker & Co." or elsewhere. Nor does he know whether he paid it to the person authorized to receive it or not, but he insists that he paid it. The Committee have not committed the folly of giving any credit to a statement so improbable upon its face, but as it raised the question, whether Mr. George W. Spates, or his namesake, the President, had received the money represented by these two receipts, it became important to ascertain by whose agency they were fabricated.

It was found upon an examination of them, that they were in the handwriting of a young man of excellent character, an expert penman, employed in the office of the Clerk of Allegany County as a recorder. Two of your committee sought an interview with him and exhibited to him the receipts, informing him at the same time of the fraudulent purpose they had been made to serve. He, at once, admitted that they were in his handwriting, and stated without any reserve his whole agency in their preparation. He had copied them at the request of Mr. Alfred Spates, upon the printed bill-heads of "H. P. Tasker & Co." furnished to him by Mr. Alfred Spates. The body of the bills and the signatures were all copied by him at the same time from a manuscript furnished by Mr. Alfred Spates. The Board will see, at once, that this disposes of the statement of Mr. George W. Spates, that they were sent to him unreceipted. They were receipted at the moment of their fabrication, and of course could never have been in Mr. George W. Spates' hands without the signature. All this does not show, with absolute certainty, that Mr. Alfred Spates received this money. But it does demonstrate with incontestible certainty, that Mr. George W. Spates received the money in the first instance and that his namesake, the President, took uncommon pains to furnish him with the means of embezzling the funds of the Company over which he presided. Your Committee are content to leave this fact of the case to the reasonable construction of intelligent men.

Fifth.—In April and May, 1869, the President undertook to procure a mud-machine and scow for the use of the Monocacy Division. They were to be built, as usual, in Cumberland, and the President considerately undertook to relieve Mr. Thomas, the Division Superintendent, from the labor and responsibility of disbursing the money and procuring the vouchers. All the materials for this large expenditure, amounting to nearly $1,600, were procured in Cumberland, and your Committee have not yet had a full opportunity of determining how many of the vouchers partake of the same character with those, with which they had already become too familiar in the same kind of expenditure. Amongst the vouchers, however, which Mr. Spates, the President, sent to Mr. Thomas and which the latter officer filed with his accounts, were two, the fraudulent character of which the Committee satisfactorily established. One of these was a bill and receipt for $108.25, apparently executed by John Snyder & Co., and in the handwriting of the same person who copied the Tasker bills, and the other a bill and receipt, apparently executed by Henry Snyder, for $350, for a scow. This was in the handwriting of an accomplished penman and from its appearance would have warranted the opinion that Mr. Henry Snyder was an extensive boat-builder, whose business warranted the employment of a first-class bookkeeper. Your Committee had the good fortune to find him and instead of an employer, he turned out to be a journeyman mechanic, engaged by the day in a boat yard. The bill and receipt purporting to be in his name was exhibited to him, and the Board will learn from his affidavit how audacious and deliberate was the fraud successfully practiced upon the Company and upon Mr. Thomas by the person who sent him this spurious voucher, to be filed by an honest man as an offset to money placed in his hands for an honest purpose. The bill and receipt of Jno. Snyder & Co. is only less a fabrication than the other in this, that it appears from his statement that he actually did a small portion of the work charged in the bill, for which he received twenty-five dollars. The rest was lost to the Company and gained, like the $350 fathered upon Henry Snyder, by the person who fabricated the receipt. As Mr. Spates received the money from Mr. Thomas and sent him these false vouchers, there can, we presume, be no reasonable doubt, who gained what the Company lost. It is due to Messrs. Mans, Shay, and Thomas, the Division Superintendents, upon whom these spurious vouchers were imposed, to say that nothing has occurred in the course of this investigation to call in question their integrity and good faith in the transactions referred to.

Sixth.—In March. 1868, the late President, in pursuance of a resolution of the Board, drew the sum of ten thousand dollars, to be expended in the condemnation of certain lands at Cumberland, which the Company undertook to acquire for the purpose of making a basin. In December following, finding it necessary to account for this sum, he filed as evidence of his payments, ten different vouchers, amounting in the whole to $10,850.79. These vouchers consisted of transcripts of the records in six inquisitions for damages, three bills for sheriffs and clerks' costs, and the receipt of Patrick Murray for $324, paid to him on account of a judgment, which he had obtained against the Company as a holder of its scrip. Five of these inquisitions, and the costs upon them, appear to be proper vouchers; and had the President been content to claim credit for what he had really paid out, the transactions might have been passed without further examination, than the very superficial one which it appears to have received at the hands of the gentlemen who then constituted the Committee on Accounts. But your Committee regret to be compelled, by a sense of duty, to present to the Board, in connection with this transaction, a successful attempt at embezzlement, which, in audacity and deliberation, it would be difficult to surpass.

In 1866, the Canal Company, at the instance and expense of the "Rose Hill Wharf Company," of Allegany, agreed to allow their corporate name to be used for the condemnation of a small parcel of land belonging to Henry Thomas Weld and wife. The damages found by the jury were $724, which were increased by charges of interest to $739. The Wharf Company promptly paid the money to the Canal Company on the 21st of September, 1866, and on the same day the Canal

Company paid the damages to the attorney of Weld. By some oversight, the counsel of the Canal Company omitted to enter a satisfaction of the judgment on the docket of the court until the 9th of December, 1868. Mr. Spates, or some one for him, ordered copies of all the inquisitions, including this one against Weld. But the record, as made out by the clerk, necessarily showed that the whole proceedings in this case had taken place in 1866, and, of course, no part of the $10,000 applicable to condemnations made or to be made in 1868, could be used to satisfy it. Before, therefore, the record was filed in the office of the Canal Company, it was carefully examined, and by a skillful change of the word *six* to *eight*, the record was made to represent an inquisition sued out and executed in 1868. And, in order to make the conformity more complete, as the sheriff by whom the original inquisition was returned in 1866, was not in office in 1868—the cautious and provident fabricator inserted the word " *late* " before the name of the sheriff of 1866, so that the officer of that day might appear in 1868 to be only executing one of his unfinished official duties. There is no evidence to show by whom the alteration and falsification of this record was made, and your Committee are content with the simple statement of the fact. The *effect* of the alteration was to leave the whole sum of $739 in the possession of Mr. Spates from March, 1868, to September, 1869, when his attention being drawn to it, he promptly refunded the money.

Seventh.—The misapplication of the funds of the Company by the part payment of a judgment founded on scrip, although it does not appear to have placed any money in the hands of Mr. Spates, was an abuse of authority, which the Committee feel called upon to notice. The payment was made in spite of representations of Mr. Roman, the counsel of the Company, who fully apprised Mr. Spates that the judgment was deferred to the liens of the State and the bondholders, and remonstrated against its payment. When we consider that there are on file in Allegany county alone, judgments against the Company founded on the same deferred liabilities, amounting to more than one hundred thousand dollars, and which are as much entitled to payment as that of Mr. Murray, the satisfaction of such a judgment, under the circumstances, was a deliberate perversion of the funds of the Company, which cannot be too severely censured.

Eighth.—In March, 1868, the Canal Company was called upon by the corporation of Cumberland to remove boats and other wrecks which had sunk in the basin at that place. The counsel of the Company, upon being applied to, expressed the opinion that the Company was not bound to remove them, but an arrangement appears to have been entered into, notwithstanding, for their removal, between the corporation of Cumberland, the Canal Company, and the Cumberland Coal and Iron Company, Mr. Spates presented to the corporation a statement showing that the whole cost, to be paid by all parties, would be $1,612, and the corporation agreed to pay $540, and the Cumberland Coal and Iron Company $160.

The Canal Company actually paid	$1,452	00
The Cumberland Coal and Iron Company	160	00
The corporation	540	00
Showing payments to amount of	$2,152	00
Deduct actual cost, according to Mr. Spates' statement	1,612	00
There remains in his hands	$ 540	00

For which he has never accounted.

Ninth.—In July and September, 1868, Mr. Spates bought from J. J. Bruce, on his own account, lumber to the value of $644.90 which he caused to be charged to and paid for by the Company, and for which he has never accounted. Explanations of these two last transactions have been brought to the attention of your Committee, but they have been examined with impartiality and candor, and have proved wholly unsatisfactory.

Although your Committee, from the direct and positive character of the evidence upon which the statements of the report rest, would be warranted in proceeding, without further delay, to take decided and peremptory steps to assert the violated rights of the Company, yet, as Mr. Spates has, in a communication to the President and Directors, desired that he may be furnished with a copy of their report, and as your Committee would heartily welcome any explanation which would remove or palliate the painful impression which these transactions have made upon their minds, they recommend that a copy of this report be furnished to Mr. Spates, and that he be informed that the Board will proceed to act upon it at their next monthly meeting, on Wednesday, the 12th of January next, at Annapolis.

(Signed) J. H. GORDON,
NEILSON POE,
WM. THOMPSON, of R.,
D. L. BISER.

In pursuance of an order submitted to the Senate by the Hon. Alfred Spates, on the eighteenth day of February, eighteen hundred and seventy, namely:

Ordered, That a Committee of three be appointed by the President, with full power and authority to send for persons and papers, to examine the books, accounts, papers and proceedings of the Chesapeake and Ohio Canal Company, and examine witnesses, under oath, to the end that a full and entire investigation may be made of the accounts of the late President of said Company, Alfred Spates, as well as all other accounts, books, papers and proceedings of the present administration of said Company, said Committee to report to the Senate at an early day, the result of its investigations.

Which was read and adopted.

The President appointed as said Committee, Senators Henry, Clarke and Sellman.

OFFICE OF THE CHESAPEAKE AND OHIO CANAL COMPANY.

To the Honorable the Committee appointed by the Senate to examine the "Books, accounts, papers and proceedings of the Canal Company."

Gentlemen :—The proceedings indicated by the order under which you were appointed will probably require the attendance of a number of the agents of the Canal Company, who are very busily engaged at this time in preparing the work for an early resumption of navigation, and for the purpose of avoiding unnecessary delay in that respect, and also for the purpose of presenting the questions raised or to be raised by this proceeding, I propose that you adopt some rules for your proceeding in the matter which may facilitate the investigation and avoid delay, and any such accumulation of expense to the State as might result from delay.

And I beg leave to suggest the following order of proceeding for your consideration :

First.—That you take up the charges made against Mr. Spates by the report of the Committee of the Canal Company, "*seriatim*," each in its order, and that the testimony relating to each charge, be kept separate from the other testimony as far as possible.

This will enable you to divide with more ease the questions of relevancy that will probably arise in offering the different parts of the testimony.

It will also enable you to examine the witnesses upon each part of the case separately, and when through with them to permit them to return to their duties again.

It will also present the different questions in a more convenient shape for examination and decision by the Senate.

Second.—I also suggest that a short-hand reporter be employed to take down the testimony of the witnesses, and report your proceedings, and that each party be furnished with a copy of the proceedings of the Committee daily while taking the testimony.

Third.—I also propose that each party shall furnish to you a list of witnesses to be summoned and examined by the Committee, and that a copy of the list so furnished by each party shall be given to the other party before the witnesses are summoned.

I also beg leave to say that the earliest day that you can name for commencing this proceeding will best suit the President and Board of Directors of the Canal Company.   J. H. GORDON,
President of the Canal Company.

Your early reply will much oblige,

Yours, truly, &c.,

J. H. GORDON.

FEBRUARY 22D, 1870.

I also send herewith a list of witnesses to be summoned in the case.

J. H. GORDON.

List of witnesses to be produced before the Special Committee of the Senate raised to investigate the official conduct of Alfred Spates, Esq., late President of the Chesapeake and Ohio Canal Company.

Thomas Sheridan..................................Cumberland, Md.
Dr. John J. Bruce.................................... "
Hiram P. Tasker..................................... "
William R. McCulley............................ "
Henry Snyder.. "
John Synder... "
J. J. McHenry....................................... "
John Patterson..................................... "

Henry McKeon, Clerk of the Corporation of Cumberland, to bring with him the original paper filed by Mr. Spates, to show the cost of removing boats from basin in March, 1868.

John Shay, Superintendent............Sharpsburg, Washington Co.
Amos Thomas, Superintendent............Adamstown, Frederick Co.
Isaac R. Maus, Superintendent.................Georgetown, D. C.
Geo. W. Spates, late Superintendent......Edward's Ferry, Montgomery Co., Maryland.
Benj. Fawcett, Clerk of Canal Company..............at Annapolis, Md.
John B. Thomas..................................House of Delegates.
Percy Roland.......................Clerk's Office, Cumberland, Md.
Patrick Murray.....................Mount Savage, Allegany Co.

[Copy of letter to Hon. J. H. Gordon.]

ANNAPOLIS, February 23d, 1870.

HON. J. H. GORDON,

President of the Chesapeake and Ohio Canal Company:

Sir :—Your communication of the 22d inst. was laid before the Special Committee to which it was addressed at a meeting held to-day, and I have been instructed by the Committee to invite you, as the representative of the Canal Company, and also Mr. Spates, to attend the sessions of the Committee, either in person or by counsel, and take part in the conduct of its investigations. I was also instructed to notify you that the Committee will require the production of all books, accounts and papers relating to or connected with the questions involved, which may be under your control as President of said Company. Direction will be given for the summoning of the witnesses named in the list furnished by you, as soon as the Sergeant-at-Arms returns to Annapolis. You will be furnished with a list of the witnesses desired by Mr. Spates in due time, after such list is handed to the Committee. No conclusion was arrived at in regard to the exact order of proceeding. A short-hand writer will be employed in accordance with your suggestion, and the Committee propose to proceed with the investigation as speedily as practicable, and with that view, will ask leave to sit, if necessary, during the sessions of the Senate.

In behalf of the Committee, I am, respectfully, &c.,

DANIEL M. HENRY,
Chairman.

OFFICE CHESAPEAKE AND OHIO CANAL CO.
ANNAPOLIS, MD., Feb. 24th, 1870.

HON. DANIEL M. HENRY,

Chairman of Committee to examine Books and Accounts of the Chesapeake and Ohio Canal Co.:

Dear Sir :—Your favor of yesterday's date was received this morning. In reply, I beg leave to say that your determination, so far as it goes, is entirely satisfactory, and I beg leave to return you my thanks for your prompt attention to the matter.

The books, papers and accounts of the Canal Company are ready at any time for the inspection of your Committee, and I would suggest that the office of the Company would be the best place for the Committee to hold its meetings while examining the books and papers. It will avoid the necessity of carrying the books and papers out of the office, and the dangers of loss or injury to them. I am compelled to leave the city to-day on important business of the Company, but any communication that you desire to make to me can be left with Mr. Fawcett, the secretary of the Company, at its office, or with Neilson Poe, esq., who will act for me in my absence.

Truly yours, &c.,

J. H. GORDON,
President Canal Company.

[Copy of Letter sent to Hon. A. Spates.]

ANNAPOLIS, Feb. 23d, 1870.

HON. ALFRED SPATES:

Sir :—By direction of the Special Committee appointed at your instance, I herewith transmit to you a list of witnesses suggested by Mr. Gordon, President of the Chesapeake and Ohio Canal Company, and request that you will furnish the Committee with a list of the witnesses to be examined on your part. I was also instructed to invite both yourself and Mr. Gordon to attend the sessions of the Committee, either in person or by counsel, and to take part in the conduct of its investigations. In behalf of the Committee,

I am, respectfully, &c.,

DANIEL M. HENRY,
Chairman.

[Copy of Letter sent to Hon. A. Spates.]

GENERAL ASSEMBLY OF MARYLAND, (SENATE,)
ANNAPOLIS, Feb. 25th, 1870.

HON. ALFRED SPATES:

Sir:—I am instructed by the Committee of Investigation appointed by order of the Senate on the 18th instant, to notify you that they are about to issue summons for the witnesses suggested by the Chesapeake and Ohio Canal Company, requiring their attendance here on Tuesday next, March 1st, and to request that you will furnish the Committee, at your earliest convenience, with a list of such witnesses as you desire to have summoned. Respectfully, &c.,

DANIEL M. HENRY,
Chairman Committee.

[Exhibit J. M. S.]

List of Witnesses summoned for Alfred Spates, Esq.

Richard M. Sprigg,
Daniel Wineow,
William Dowden,
C. Slack,
John Humbird,
Asahel Willison,

N. J. Berston,
John M. Resley,
George Hughes,
William Wineow,
Francis Smeltzer,
James Noonan.

JAMES T. BLACKISTONE, ESQ.,
Sergeant-at-Arms:

Please summons the above named parties as witnesses for A. Spates, Esq.

J. M. SCHLEY,
February 28th, 1870.   *For the People.*

Memorandum.

Mr. Spates did not make any reply in writing to either of the foregoing letters. He left, shortly after he received the letter of 25th February, for Cumberland, and on 28th February the Chairman of the Committee received from the Sergeant-at-Arms a telegram from Cumberland, where he was at that time engaged in summoning the witnesses suggested by Messrs. Gordon and Poe, stating that Col. Spates had furnished him with a list of such witnesses as he desired, (which list is herewith filed, marked "Exhibit J. M. S.,") and requesting the direction of the Committee as to whether he should summon them. The Chairman, desiring to save the expense and trouble of another trip to Cumberland, and seeing no reason to the contrary, immediately sent a dispatch to the Sergeant-at-Arms, directing him to summon them, which he accordingly did. On his return the list was filed, at the first meeting of the Committee, with the Clerk, where it was open to the inspection of all the parties interested at any time. This explanation is made to show why the Committee did not furnish Mr. Gordon with a list of the defendant's witnesses before they were summoned, and why, after the return of the list, it became unnecessary for them to do so. A copy of the list could have been obtained from the Clerk at any time. This explanation was made in substance to Messrs. Gordon and Poe in committee.

DANIEL M. HENRY,
Chairman.

OFFICE CHESAPEAKE AND OHIO CANAL CO.,
ANNAPOLIS, MD., February 25, 1870.

Dear Sir :—I enclose to you a list of the witnesses whose testimony in considered material in connection with the report presented on the 9th of December, 1869, by the Committee on Accounts, to the President and Directors of the Chesapeake and Ohio Canal Company in relation to the official conduct of the late President.

I have, with a view to the saving of time and expense, confined this list to such witnesses as can testify to the particular allegations of that report, and have not made provision for any enquiry beyond that which necessarily grows out of the report.

With great respect,
Your obedient servant,
NELSON POE.

HON. D. M. HENRY, Chairman, &c.

To JAMES T. BLACKISTONE,

Sergeant-at-Arms of the Senate of Maryland, Greeting:

Sir :—The Special Committee appointed by the Senate of Maryland, with power and authority to send for persons and papers, to examine the books, accounts, papers and proceedings of the Chesapeake and Ohio Canal Company, and examine witnesses under oath, to the end that a full and entire investigation may be made of the accounts of the late President of said Company, Alfred Spates, as well as all other accounts, books, papers and proceedings of the present administration of said Company, hereby command that you summon the following named witnesses to appear in person before the said Committee, at 9 o'clock A. M., on Tuesday, the first day of March, 1870, in the city of Annapolis, all excuses and delays set apart, and that you have then and there this writ.

Names of Witnesses.

Thomas Sheridan..Cumberland, Md.
Dr. John J. Bruce ....   "
Hiram P. Tasker..   "
Wm. R. McCulley...   "
Henry Snyder...   "
John Snyder..   "
J. J. McHenry..   "
John Patterson...   "
Henry McKeon, Clerk of corporation, to bring with him the original paper filed by Mr. Spates to show the cost of removing boats from basin in March, 1868.
John Shay, Superintendent.................Sharpsburg, Washington Co.
Amos Thomas, Superintendent................Adamstown, Frederick Co.
Isaac R. Mans, Superintendent.........................Georgetown, D. C.
Geo. W. Spates, late Superintendent..Edward's Ferry, Montgomery, Co.
Benj. Fawcett, Clerk of Canal Co........ ....Annapolis, Md.
John B. Thomas, House of Delegates........................Annapolis.
Percy Roland, Clerk's Office.................................Cumberland.
Patrick Murray............................Mount Savage, Allegany Co.
Theodore W. Evans.
Ezekiel Male.

DAN'L M. HENRY,
Chair. Sp. Committee.

Annapolis, Feb'y 25, 1870.

Office Chesapeake and Ohio Canal Co.
Annapolis, Md., February 28, 1870.

D. M. Henry, Esq.,

Chairman, &c., &c.:

Dear Sir :—In addition to the witnesses to be summoned before the Special Committee, of which you are chairman, I beg to ask for subpœnas for

Lloyd Lowe..Cumberland.
Clement A. Peck.............................near Georgetown, D. C.
Hon. Wm. Veirs Bouic.....................Rockville, Montgomery Co.
Richard M. Sprigg..Cumberland.

With great respect,
Your obedient servant,
NELSON POE.

OFFICE OF THE CHESAPEAKE AND OHIO CANAL CO.,
ANNAPOLIS, MD., March 3, 1870.
To D. M. HENRY, Esq.,
Chairman, &c., &c. :

Sir:—We desire a subpœna for Geo. W. Spates, Edwards' Ferry, Montgomery county, Md., returnable immediately, to testify before the Special Committee of the Senate raised upon the motion of Alfred Spates, Esq.

J. H. GORDON,
NELSON POE.

OFFICE CHESAPEAKE AND OHIO CANAL CO.,
ANNAPOLIS, MD., March 29th, 1870.

Additional witnesses to be summoned by the Investigating Committee in the case of Alfred Spates.

From Cumberland—James Terrell, Wm. Devecmon, Patrick Kennedy, James Mulligan, James Noonan, Matthias Snow, Jacob Brengle, P. J. Cahill, Thomas Ried, Henry Dryer.

J. H. GORDON.

ANNAPOLIS, March ———, 1870.
JAMES T. BLAKISTONE, Esq.,
Sergeant-at-Arms :

Sir :—You are hereby commanded to summon Lloyd Lowe, Cumberland; Clement A. Peck, near Georgetown, D. C.; Richard M. Sprigg, Cumberland, to be and appear here, immediately, before the Committee of the Senate to investigate the charges preferred against A. Spates, late President Chesapeake and Ohio Canal Company. Fail not at your peril.

DAN'L M. HENRY,
Chairman Special Committee.

ANNAPOLIS, March 9th, 1870.
JAMES T. BLAKISTONE, Esq.,
Sergeant-at-Arms :

Sir :—You are hereby commanded to summon James Terrell, Wm. Devecmon, Patrick Kennedy, James Mulligan, James Noonan, Mathias Snow, Jacob Brengle, P. J. Cahill, Thomas Ried, Henry Dryer, Cumberland, to be and appear here, immediately, to testify before Senate Investigating Committee in the "Spates' Investigation." Fail not at your peril. By order of Committee.

DAN'L M. HENRY,
Chairman Special Committee.

ANNAPOLIS, March 3d, 1870.

JAMES T. BLACKISTONE, ESQ.,

  Sergeant-at-Arms:

Sir :—You are hereby commanded to summon George W. Spates, Edward's Ferry, Montgomery county, to be and appear here immediately before the Committee of the Senate, to investigate the charges preferred against A. Spates, late President Chesapeake and Ohio Canal Company. Fail not at your peril.

        DANIEL M. HENRY,
        Chairman Special Committee.

MARCH 17th, 1870.

TO JAMES T. BLACKISTONE,

 Sergeant-at-Arms of the Senate of Maryland, Greeting :

Sir :—You are hereby commanded to summon and bring before the Senate Investigating Committee, "in the Spates investigation,"

Neil J. Berston,	Casper Bringer,
William R. McCulley,	Theodore W. Evans;
E. Male,	John Patterson.

All excuses and delays sit apart. Hereof fail not at your peril.

        DANIEL M. HENRY,
        Chairman Special Committee.

CUMBERLAND, March 18th, 1870.

THE HONORABLE T. BLACKISTONE :

It is my candid opinion, as a physician, that if Mr. Neal Berston is removed to Annapolis, it will be the death of him. He is not in a condition to be taken from home.

        GEORGE C. PERRY, M. D.

List of witnesses summoned by James T. Blackistone, Esq., Sergeant-at-Arms, to appear before the Senate Investigating Committee, by order of the Committee:

Thomas Sheridan,	John Patterson,
Dr. John J. Bruce,	Patrick Kennedy,
Hiram P. Tasker,	Matthias Snow,
William R. McCulley,	James Terrell,
Henry Snyder,	Lloyd Lowe,
John Snyder,	Jacob Brengle,
J. J. McHenry,	Richard M. Sprigg,
John Patterson,	Daniel Wineow,
Henry McKeon,	William Dowden,
John Shay,	C. Slack,
Amos Thomas,	John Humbird,
Isaac R. Mans,	Asahel Willison,
George W. Spates,	N. J. Berston,
Benjamin Fawcett,	John M. Resley,
John B. Thomas,	George Hughes,
Percy Roland,	William Wineow,
Patrick Murray,	Francis Smeltzer,
Theodore W. Evans,	James Noonan,
Ezekiel A. Mail,	A. I. Berston,
Clement A. Peck,	Caspar Brinker,
Neil J. Berston,	A. K. Stake,
Casper Bringer,	Sydney I. Wales,
Wm. R. McCully,	Gov. Oden Bowie,
Theodore W. Evans,	Dr. W. McPherson.
E. Male,	Judge Wm. V. Bowie.

WEDNESDAY, March 2d, 1870.

The Committee met at 10 o'clock, A. M. Present—Mr. Henry, Chairman, and Messrs. Clark and Sellman; Mr. Schley, counsel for Mr. Spates, Mr. Spates, and Messrs. Poe and Gordon.

The Chairman stated the Committee was organized and ready to proceed with the investigation, and that the Sergeant-at-Arms had made his report in regard to the witnesses.

Mr. Schley thought before proceeding farther it was well to know whether they were fighting anybody, or fighting the wind. In the first place, he would ask that the official report of the Chesapeake and Ohio Canal Company be produced, as they had no right to suppose the newspaper reports were a true copy. He would then ask by whose authority that report was put in the newspaper; whether the Board of Public Works authorized the report to be published; then, whether the Chesapeake and Ohio Canal Company, or the Board, authorized the President or Directors to hand the list of summonses to the Committee ; then, whether the Chesapeake and Ohio Canal Company have passed resolutions authorizing them to be represented by counsel. If not, he would deny the authority of the President, as President, or the Director, as a Director, to appear on the part of that Company. They did not shrink from an investigation, but as the resolutions offered by Mr. Spates show, desired it, but desired to know whether the two gentlemen present were authorized by the Company to represent them, or whether they appeared in their individual capacity. If not authorized, those gentlemen have no right to appear as counsel for the Canal Company. The Company should take action in an official manner, and they should appear in an official capacity.

Mr. Gordon said he had simply to say that a motion had been made in the Senate by the Senator from Allegany, stating the charges published in the Baltimore American were gotten up for the purpose of persecution by the parties who had made that report, and that he demanded an investigation, and was ready to prove those charges false. He stated at the same time he had sought an opportunity to show that the charges were false, and we now come forward as we think we have a right to do.

As members of the Committee on Accounts, we felt that it was due to Mr. Spates that an opportunity should be presented to him at the earliest day possible, to have this matter examined and explained, and before that Committee proceeded to Cumberland they directed that a letter should be written to Mr. Spates informing him of the time the Committee would be in Cumberland for the purpose of going into this examination, and Mr. Poe was directed to write the letter and give him full information of all points to which the Committee intended to direct their attention in the investigation of the accounts. This letter he wrote.

Mr. Schley said what he desired to know was, whether the gentlemen were here in an official capacity to represent the Canal Company, and bind it by their action, or as private prosecutors. If they did not appear for the Canal Company, that Company may repudiate their acts.

Mr. Gordon said he would state the facts in connection with the matter, and would then leave it for the Committee to decide whether they had a right to be present or not: he did not undertake to forestall the opinion of the Committee, or to anticipate the result of the investigation. We invited Mr. Spates to appear before the Committee, which he declined to do for reasons which will appear in his letter. The Committee then proceeded to make such examination as best we could into the matter. They called before them certain employees of the Company, and prepared a report. They received a communication from Mr. Spates, stating that inasmuch as he had not appeared to take part in the examination, he should have a copy of the report. The letter, with his signature, was in the possession of the Company. A copy of the report was furnished him by mail. On the 12th of January the Committee again met, at Annapolis, of which he had notice. He did not appear, or make any application for further time. We still held the matter over, waiting still and hoping still that he might come forward and make some explanation, but nothing was done. In the meantime these matters had been spoken of, and the stockholders becoming aware of this investigation, the report was called for. We had a meeting on the 17th of February, and the report was made. After it was made the Committee was severely censured for having kept the matter quiet, and not having pushed it to an issue. I, for one, determined that these things should not be complained of any further, and being called on by a reporter, told him I had no objections to his getting a copy of the report.

These are the facts, gentlemen; the balance you know, as to the formation of the Committee and the authority under which you are acting. The Board took no action, but the individual members all concurred that Mr. Poe and myself should attend this investigation and see that the Committee got all the information they desired, and had access to the books and papers of the Canal Company.

Mr. Poe.—Mr. Chairman, the inquiry of the counsel of Mr. Spates is addressed not merely to the President but to myself, and as it is a proper one I think it is incumbent upon me as an individual member of the directory of the Chesapeake and Ohio Canal Company to show why I am here. I should never have been here of my own motion. I am not a prosecutor of Mr. Spates now, at any time or in any sense. I do not desire to be and do not intend to be, but the Committee will recollect that in Mr. Spates' remarks concerning the report of the Committee of the Chesapeake and Ohio Canal Company, in reference to his conduct, of which Committee I am chairman, he said it was prompted by personal and political rancor and malice, and he said so in strong language. I am a stranger to any such motives or feelings, and feel it incumbent upon me to ask that I may be present to show that I acted in good faith and in the sense of public duty. I disclaim as entirely inapplicable to myself the slightest imputation of malice towards Mr. Spates now or at any time. My acquaintance with Mr. Spates, although it covers many years, was never intimate or familiar, or accompanied with one solitary circumstance which was inconsistent with the utmost good will towards him. There is no rivalry between Mr. Spates and myself. Our paths lie in opposite directions. They do not converge anywhere; they diverge everywhere.

The attempt to bring Mr. Spates before our Committee, so that he might give us the benefit of his explanations, has been referred to. I took an active part in the measures to bring him before the Committee, but he declined in his letter on the ground that we had prejudged his case. Now, Mr. President, I hold that that was a very unjust intimation, but I do not quarrel with him for having made it. But he has now an opportunity of making those explanations before a tribunal which he cannot say has prejudged his case. He now stands in the presence of judges indulgent, tolerant, and I hope, within the constraint of conscience and duty, even favorable to him. Let him supply here to-day the omission of which he was guilty when he failed to come before our Committee. Let him take up the report of the Committee on Accounts and their charges in their series and let us have the benefit of his explanations. I speak of his judges, but can speak with more certainty of his accusers, and declare that when he furnishes indisputable evidence of his innocence and proves that we have committed an error and done him injustice, no pride of opinion shall induce me to hesitate one moment in giving him a full vindication.

The Committee on Accounts was raised to investigate the official conduct of Mr. Spates. That Committee on the 9th of December met. The report of that Committee was, upon a full consideration, unanimously adopted by the Board and was communicated to Mr. Spates, and although the Board has had many meetings since, he has never vouchsafed to take the slightest notice of it. In regard to a point which seems to be of consequence, I will state that two meetings of the stockholders have transpired since the report was agreed upon. Mr. Corcoran, one of the largest stockholders, offered a resolution calling upon the Directors of the Chesapeake and Ohio Canal Company, to furnish the report, which was done, read in the presence of the Stockholders, and remains in their archives as their official act.

Mr. Schley stated in reply that he had advised Mr. Spates that his self-respect forbade him from appearing before a Committee which had prejudged his case. (Adjourned until 7½ o'clock, P. M.)

Mr. Schley—Stated he had advised Mr. Spates not to appear before any Committee who had prejudged his case.

Committee then adjourned to meet again at 7 P. M.

7½ P. M., MARCH 2d, 1870.

Committee met pursuant to adjournment.

Present—Mr. Henry, Chairman, Messrs. Clarke and Sellman; Mr. Spates and Mr. Schley, his counsel; Mr. Gordon, President, and Mr. Poe, Director, Chesapeake and Ohio Canal Company.

Mr. Henry, Chairman—Stated that the Committee had examined the books of the Company, and found that the proceedings of the Committee had been endorsed by the Board of Directors, and that the report had been made with their full knowledge and consent, though it did not appear that these gentlemen had been authorized by the Board to appear. If Mr. Spates, by his counsel, still objects, let him reduce his objections to writing and file them, and we shall be pleased to hear both sides argue this question.

On motion of Mr. Clarke, time was given Mr. Spates' counsel to prepare and file his objections.

Committee then adjourned to meet at 9 o'clock to-morrow.

MARCH 3d, 1870, 9 A. M.

Committee met pursuant to adjournment.

Present—Mr. Henry, Chairman, Messrs. Clarke and Sellman; Mr. Spates and Mr. Schley, his counsel; Mr. Gordon, President, and Mr. Poe, Director, Chesapeake and Ohio Canal Company.

Mr. Gordon—Desired to know whether certain witnesses were here properly, not having been summoned by order of Committee, but were here by request of President of Canal Company.

The Chair—Decided said witnesses would be recognized.

Mr. Schley—Then offered his written objections, and proceeded to enforce the same (paper marked No. 10) with an argument, all going to prove, that from the charter, by-laws, rules and regulations of this Canal Company, the President can, in no case, act without the authority of the Board.

Mr. Gordon—I think this all arises from a misconception of this whole case. We do not appear here as plaintiffs. It is merely to enable the gentlemen here to meet these charges, made on the books of the Canal Company, and enable him to purge himself of them.

Referred to *Curtis' Digest*,   12 *Wheaton*,
Bank vs. Dandridge,   vol. 7, p. 69;
Elysville Manufacturing Co. vs.   5th *Md. Reports.*
           vs. *Young*,   12th *Md. Reports.*

Committee then retired for consultation.

Mr. Henry, Chairman, upon re-assembling, said—We have thought over this matter, and conclude that the gentlemen should be present as parties interested. In the remarks of the Senator, calling for this investigation, he alluded to these gentlemen in their official capacity. We therefore think they have the right to be present. We will now proceed to the investigation.

Committee then adjourned to meet at 4½ P. M.

MARCH 3D, 1870, 4½ P. M.

Committee met pursuant to adjournment.

Present—Mr. Henry, Chairman, Messrs. Clarke and Sellman; Mr. Spates, his counsel, Mr. Schley; Mr. Gordon, President, and Mr. Poe, Director, Chesapeake and Ohio Canal Company.

[Paper No. 10.]

Alfred Spates, by his attorney, J. M. Schley, comes before your honorable Committee, appointed by an order of the Senate of Maryland to investigate certain charges published in the "Baltimore American," made by a committee of the Chesapeake and Ohio Canal Board, against the said Alfred Spates, former President of said Canal Company, contesting and denying the right of the President or any Director to appear for or represent said Canal Company before your honorable Committee, without first having obtained authority from the President and Directors of said Company so to do, as it appears to your honorable Committee, by an inspection of the books of said Company, no such power has been delegated to said President or any Director, by any resolution or order of said President and Directors, or a majority of them, to represent said Canal Company before your honorable Committee in said investigation. The said Alfred Spates, by his attorney, contends that no such power as is now claimed by said President, or any Director, is given directly or indirectly, by any provision of the charter, by-laws, rules or regulations of said Company. As will appear by reference to sections three and four, and all sections in said charter where reference is made to the powers of said Board, the words "President and Directors" are used. And the said Alfred Spates, by his attorney, requests that said authority shall first be obtained by a resolution of said President and Directors. The charter under which said President and Directors derive their powers was originally passed by the State of Virginia, and adopted by the States of Maryland and Pennsylvania and the Congress of the United States, each and all jealously guarding against the exercise of any powers by the President or any Director, by virtue of said charter, except specially delegated by said "President and Directors, or a majority of them," by resolution or order, recorded in their proceedings.

CHARGE No. 1.

THURSDAY, March 3d, 1870.

The Committee met at 4.30 o'clock P. M.

Present—Mr. Henry, Chairman, and Messrs. Clarke and Sellman; Mr. Spates, Mr. Schley, his counsel; Mr. Gordon, President, and Mr. Poe, Director of the Chesapeake and Ohio Canal Company.

ISAAC R. MANS was called and sworn.

Examination by Mr. Poe.

Ques. What is your occupation?
Ans. Superintendent of the Georgetown Division of the Chesapeake and Ohio Canal Company.

Ques. How long have you been Superintendent of the Georgetown Division?
Ans. The last time I was appointed on the 1st of December, 1866.

Ques. Did you in the months of November or December, 1867, send any money to Alfred Spates, Esq., President of the Chesapeake and Ohio Canal Company; if so, how much did you send?

Ans. About December, 1867, I sent to Col. Spates, at Cumberland, by Adams Express, $800, to pay for an ice breaker.

Ques. Did you receive any vouchers from Mr. Spates for the expenditure of such money; if so, what were they?

Ans. I received from him a voucher for that ice breaker amounting to $800, which I returned in my abstract to the office.

Ques. Is that the abstract you speak of, (marked exhibit No. 11, I. R. M.)?

Ans. That is the abstract.

Ques. Look at that abstract and tell the Committee whether the vouchers, signed Thomas Sheridan and John Touber, were filed with that abstract?

Ans. Both vouchers were filed with the abstract?

Ques. Look at the papers marked Sheridan, No. 11, and Touber, No. 11; were they the vouchers that were filed, and from whom did you receive them?

Ans. I received them from Col. Spates, if they were the vouchers that were returned by me in the office. After they passed out of my hands I had nothing more to do with them.

Ques. Look at the letters marked A. S. 1, A. S. 2 and A. S. 3, and tell us in whose handwriting they are, and whether they were received by you?

Ans. They were received by me from Col. Spates, and are in his handwriting.

Ques. Where did you get the $800 you sent to Col. Spates?

Ans. I am not certain whether I got the money from J. McHenry Hollingsworth, collector at Georgetown, or W. S. Ringgold, secretary. It was the Canal Company's money. My impression is that I got it from Col. Hollingsworth.

CUMBERLAND, MD., Nov. 25th, 1867.

ISAAC R. MANS,

Sir:—I will write you in a few days when to come for the icebreaker. It is being built in the very best manner, and ironed strong. It can be used for a scow as well as an ice breaker. You will have to send men and horses to take it down. You will have to send $800.00 in money. I will have it all ready, receipts for you and all. Send the men to me. I have written Mr. Ringgold to give you $800.00 to pay for this ice breaker, over and above what you will require for other expenses upon your Division. I hope you have had the other ice breakers on your Division fixed up, and ready in case of ice. The water is to be drawn off the Canal on the 20th of December, except the lower or Georgetown Division. I hope the stone is in at the outlet lock—that you are at work at the hotel or house at Great Falls—the lock gates and locks being repaired, and all things on your Division ready to be put in order, or being now put in order. You have lock gate timber by this time, plenty, I suppose. I would like to know how things are on your Division, and what is being done, and what has been done, &c., as I gave you full instructions when I last saw you.

Your attention will oblige, yours, &c.,

ALFRED SPATES.

P. S.—I will write when to send for the ice breaker, or I might be able to send it down. I will let you know which. You must get the money the first next month to pay for it—it is cash.

A. S.

CUMBERLAND, MD., November 30, 1867.

ISAAC R. MANS,

Sir:—I have started the ice breaker to you at Georgetown by Mr. M. Rosworm. Upon the receipt of the ice breaker I have given him an order to you for *one hundred dollars* for taking it to Georgetown in four days. I made the calculation that it would of cost you about this amount for three men and horses eight days, and perhaps got in the ice. I have put on it a new good cooking stove, all complete. It is the best built ice breaker that was ever on the Canal; well built, well ironed, lined with oak, in fact a double boat, to be used for a scow and ice breaker both. The cabin comes off, with extra plank to fit in, &c. It is an elegant boat, 60 feet long, &c.

You will please send me by *Adams & Company's* Express, to Cumberland, Md., eight hundred and twenty-six dollars, ($826.00,) $800.00 to pay for the ice breaker, and $26.00 for cooking stove and fixtures. I will pay for the breaker—get the proper vouchers for it and the cooking stove, and send them to you by mail as soon as I get the money. You will please write me how you are getting along with your work at the Great Falls, and on your entire Division. I wish to know at once. Have you bought the house at the Chain Bridge.

Respectfully, &c.,

ALFRED SPATES.

CUMBERLAND, December 2d, 1867.

I. R. MANS,

Sir:—Yours of Nov. 30th came to hand containing draft for *eight hundred*, to pay for ice breaker, &c. I will send receipts to-morrow. I have sent the breaker by M. Rosworm. I put on it a good cooking stove and fixtures; it is an elegant boat, to be used for a scow as well as ice breaker; in fact, it is a double boat, lined with oak and well ironed.

Respectfully, &c.,

ALFRED SPATES.

Cross-Examination by Mr. Schley.

Ques. You received the ice breaker with the stove and and fixtures on it?

Ans. Yes, sir.

Ques. Did I understand you to say the paper marked "Sheridan No. 11" was the paper you filed at the Canal office?

Ans. The paper sent to me I filed at the office. I do not undertake to say that is the paper.

Ques. Did you take it to the office yourself?

Ans. Yes, sir. I know nothing of the signature or hand writing of that paper.

Ques. You say the letters marked A. S., 1, 2 and 3, were received by you from Col. Spates?

Ans. Yes, sir.

Ques. How did they get in possession of the Canal office?

Ans. I was summoned before the Investigating Committee and requested by Mr. Poe and Mr. Thompson to produce those letters.

Ques. Was it a written or verbal summons?

Ans. A written summons.

Ques. What have you done with the summons?

Ans. I do not know whether I have it or not.

Ques. Who served it on you?

Ans. I cannot say. I think it was a letter. I do not know whether written by Mr. Thompson or not, requesting me to call on G. W. Spates and get him to go with me to Rockville to appear before an Investigating Committee.

Ques. Was that all of the letter?

Ans. That was pretty much all that was in the letter.

Ques. How came you to bring those letters before the Committee?

Ans. I was requested to do so by Mr. Poe.

Ques. How did Mr. Poe know you had the letters?

Ans. He wanted to know how I came into possession of those vouchers. I told him they were sent from Cumberland, and he requested me to produce the letters.

Re-Examination by Mr. Poe.

Ques. Is that list of vouchers in your hand-writing?

Ans. They are in my son's hand-writing.

Ques. Were the words Thomas Sheridan written by him?

Ans. They were.

Ques. Were those words written at the time the abstract was made out?
Ans. Yes.
Ques. Did you examine it yourself?
Ans. Yes, sir.
Ques. Did the vouchers correspond with the abstract when you made it out and returned it to the office?
Ans. Yes, sir.
Ques. Thomas Sheridan was then written at the time the abstract was made, in December, 1867?
Ans. Yes, sir.
Ques. That paper was returned to the Canal office by the endorsement on the 6th of January, 1868?
Ans. Yes, sir.

Re-Cross-Examination by Mr. Schley.

Ques. You filed this paper in January?
Ans. I returned it to the office after I made it out.
Ques. This is your November, 1867, statement?
Ans. Then I must have returned it in December, because on the 1st day of the month we would get the money to pay off. Then I would go up the line and pay off, and then make out the abstract and take it to the office.
Ques. When ought the paper to have been filed?
Ans. I ought to have returned it by the 20th of December, but sometimes it is sooner and sometimes later.
Ques. Were you present when your son made it out?
Ans. Yes, sir.
Ques. Was this piece of paper attached to the abstract at the time it was made out?
Ans. Yes, sir. There were not lines enough to hold all the bills. In many cases we have to paste a piece on to extend it down. Sometimes we have few bills and sometimes a good many.

By Mr. Clarke.

Ques. The parties you pay do not sign this roll?
Ans. They did not then; they do now.
Ques. What is the object of putting Thos. Sheridan's name there?
Ans. To account for the money I paid him.
Ques. At the time this abstract was made it was not the usual mode to take a man's signature on the abstract for the money paid him?
Ans. No; they were taken on the vouchers.

(Mr. Schley called the attention of the Committee to the endorsement, stating that the paper was examined and approved by the Company on January 16th.)

I. R. MANS.

THOMAS SHERIDAN was called and sworn.

Examination by Mr. Poe.

Question. Where do you reside, and what is your occupation?

Answer. I live in Cumberland. I am superintendent of a boat yard, and a lumber yard, and also superintend the shipping of coal.

Ques. Where did you reside, and what was your occupation in the year 1867?

Ans. I had the same place of abode, and the same occupation.

Ques. Look at the papers purporting to be a receipt by Thomas Sheridan for building, ironing, painting and furnishing one ice breaker for use of Georgetown Division for $800, and state whether any part thereof is in your handwriting?

Ans. No part of this is in my handwriting, but I see by the date that about that time we did some work for the Canal Company.

Ques. Whom do you mean by we?

Ans. I am manager for Henry Thomas Weld, and I used the word in that connection. On the 4th of December we finished some work for the Canal Company, which amounted to $209.14.

Ques. Were you paid for it?

Ans. Yes, sir; by Mr. Sprigg, the Superintendent of that Division of the Canal.

Ques. State whether you ever furnished to any division of the Canal Company, any of its officers or agents, an ice-breaker, or received any money therefor?

Ans. No, sir; at no time.

Qus. How long have you lived in Allegany?

Ans. Since 1839.

Ques. Do you know of any other person of your name engaged in boat-building at any time?

Ans. I do not. I have a son named Thomas Sheridan. who is a clerk in the office of Mr. Weld—is not a boat-builder. He is a boy.

Cross-Examination by Mr. Schley.

Ques. Do you know how many boats were built by the Canal Company in 1867?

Ans. I do not. I know they were building one at the time we did this work for them, from the fact that the one they were building was the model, and I had to cross the channel to see the model. They may have built more.

Ques. Did you receive the $209.14 spoken of?

Ans. I was in the office when it was paid to Mr. P. J. Cahill, Mr. Weld's clerk.

Ques. Did you as agent for Mr. Weld contract with Mr. Sprigg to build the ice breaker?

Ans. I did.

Ques. Then the hands you had were employed by the Canal Company?

Ans. They were not employed by the Canal Company. They were my hands. I worked them on the boat and in the yard.

Ques. Who paid the money for the hands to Mr. Cahill?

Ans. Mr. Sprigg.

Ques. Whom did Mr. Cahill pay it to?

Ans. He put it in the safe.

Ques. Who paid the hands?

Ans. Mr. Cahill paid the hands on the regular pay day—the 15th of the month. The bill of $209.14 was paid either on the third or fourth of December, 1867. The items are for $69\frac{1}{4}$ days' work, at $2.75 per day, 56 pounds of oakum at 20 cents, and 10 gallons of pitch at 75 cents. Mr. Sprigg paid this bill in our office and took a receipt for it.

Ques. Did the Canal Company pay any of the men?

Ans. On the last day Mr. Sprigg said he was in a hurry to get the boat, and brought some four or five of his own hands and put them to work along with my men to finish the boat. I took account only of the men employed by me.

By Mr. Poe.

Ques. Mr. Sprigg, the Superintendent of the Cumberland Division, was at that time building an ice breaker with the Company's hands?

Ans. He was. He had one on the stocks at that time.

(Mr. Schley offered a paper marked "R. M. Sprigg, No. 11," to prove that Mr. Sprigg built two ice breakers in November, 1867, for which he was paid $1,600; which paper was examined and approved by the Committee on Accounts in January.)

By Mr. Gordon.

Ques. Do you recollect the names of the men who worked for you at that time?

Ans. I do not at that particular time.

Ques. Did you witness the vouchers for the payment of the men?

Ans. I witnessed them in blank, at the request of Mr. Sprigg, having confidence that he would do nothing but what was right.

By Mr. Schley.

Ques. Did I understand you to say that this money was paid directly to Mr. Cahill, and that Mr. Cahill gave Mr. Sprigg a receipt for the money?

Ans. Yes, sir.

Ques. And then you signed the receipts in blank?

Ans. Mr. Sprigg made the plea that the officers of the Company would require the names of the men working on those boats, and in order to have the receipts of the men, produced those vouchers, and to the best of my knowledge, I witnessed them in blank.

Ques. How did Mr. Sprigg get the number of days worked by the men?

Ans. He got it from the office of Mr. Weld.

Ques. Did you see that the number of days on the receipt was correct before it passed from Mr. Cahill to Mr. Sprigg?

Ans. I was standing at the desk when Mr. Cahill was drawing the receipt, but did not take it out of his hand to see if it was correct.

Ques. How did Mr. Sprigg get at the number of days your hands worked?

Ans. There was a foreman who kept the time of the men and returned it to the office.

Ques. How much did the hands get?

Ans. I cannot tell what each man got without examining the books of the office. They received from $2 to $2.50.

Ques. Did they not pay you a bonus of 25 cents on each hand?

Ans. The profit I received might have been more than that on their labor. I do not call it a bonus.

By Mr. Clarke.

Ques. Mr. Sprigg had nothing to do with the payment of the men?

Ans. Mr. Weld paid the men. They were not under Mr. Sprigg's supervision.

By Mr. Poe.

Ques. This work was on an ice breaker which the Canal Company was building?

Ans. It was for one which they were building in Mr. Weld's yard.

By Mr. Schley.

Ques. In what month did you sign your name as a witness to the blank vouchers?

Ans. I think it was at the time the money was paid.

By Mr. Poe.

Ques. What did Mr. Spates say to you in regard to your building an ice breaker for the Company?

Ans. On last Monday he told me that what I had stated in my affidavit before the Canal Committee was perfectly right, "and," said he, "I would have taken your simple word for it. I never said you built that boat. There are more Tom Sheridans than one. You and I have always been friends." "Yes," said I, "I have a son called Tom Sheridan."

By Mr. Schley.

Ques. Did he not say if the Committee had gone on a little farther they would have seen the explanation of it?

Ans. Yes; he said if they had turned over another leaf of the book they would have seen the whole thing explained.

By Mr. Poe.

Ques. Has Mr. Spates said anything to you, since you came here, to dissuade you from testifying before this Committee.

Ans. I do not think he has in a direct manner.

Ques. Did he in an indirect way?

Ans. I might have been wrong in my inference. "You and I" he said, "have always been friends."

By Mr. Clarke.

Ques. Have you ever had any dishonest transactions with Mr. Spates?

Ans. I have not.

THOMAS SHERIDAN.

CHARGE No. 3.

FRIDAY, March 4, 1870.

The Committee met this day at 9 A. M., pursuant to adjournment.

Present—Messrs. Henry, (Chairman,) Clarke and Sellman; also Messrs. Spates, Schley, (his attorney,) Gordon and Poe.

ISAAC R. MANS was recalled.

By Mr. Poe, conducting Examination-in-Chief.

Ques. Were you the Superintendent of the Georgetown Division in October, 1868?

Ans. I was.

Ques. Look at the paper now shown you, (marked Charge No. 3 I. R. Mans, Oct., 1868,) being an estimate for ordinary expenses and work authorized to be done, and state whether you received from the Canal Company the sum which appeared to be required by that estimate?

Ans. Yes, sir; I received the amount the paper calls for.

Ques. Did you pay any part of that money to Mr. Alfred Spates, and, if so, how much?

Ans. I paid him four hundred dollars ($400) of it.

Ques. Did Mr. Spates send to you a voucher for the sum which you thus paid him, and, if so, what did you do with it?

Ans. I returned it in the office, and credited myself with it on the abstract.

Ques. Look at the receipt for $400, signed J. J. Bruce, and dated Nov. 9th, 1869, (marked J. J. Bruce, $400,) and state whether that is the voucher sent to you by Mr. Spates?

Ans. I think that is it, sir.

Ques. Look at your abstract for October, 1868, (marked Charge No. 3, I. R. Mans, Oct., 1868,) and state whether the said receipt signed by J. J. Bruce, (marked J. J. Bruce, $400,) was filed by you with that abstract, and whether the abstract is in your handwriting?

Ans. The receipt was filed with the abstract. Most of the abstract is in my handwriting.

Ques. Is that particular voucher, J. J. Bruce, $400, entered on the abstract, and is that entry in your handwriting?

Ans. It is so entered, and is in my handwriting.

Ques. Was that abstract made out at or about the time of receiving the receipt of Mr. Bruce?

Ans. It was.

Cross-Examination by Mr. Schley.

Ques. Did you get the scow?
Ans. I did.

Ques. What use did you put it to?
Ans. It was used for the bottom of a house boat.

Ques. You received it from Cumberland?
Ans. I did, sir.

Ques. Have you got it now?
Ans. I have.

Ques. Is it a good boat?
Ans. It is.

Ques. What use did you make of it after the house was put on it?
Ans. It was used as a boarding-house for the hands.

Ques. Did you ever receive any notification after you filed this paper that it had been examined and passed by the Committee on Accounts?
Ans. I never heard anything more of that paper after it went out of my hands until I was summoned before the Committee.

Ques. Do not you always know when you make your returns to the office whether they are approved or not?
Ans. The Secretary does not notify me, but I know they are approved when I do not hear anything to the contrary.

(Mr. Schley offered as evidence the endorsement on the abstract, filed November 20th. "Examined and approved, February 2d, 1869, (signed) John B. Thomas and Esau Pickerell.")

I. R. MANS.

Dr. John J. Bruce sworn.

By Mr. Poe.

Ques. Are you a dealer in lumber, doing business in Cumberland?
Ans. I am.

Ques. Look at the bill and receipt for lumber, amounting to $1,257.10, and signed by you, (marked Charge No. 3, J. J. Bruce, $1,257.) State whether the lumber therein charged for was sold to to the Chesapeake and Ohio Canal Company, and paid for by that Company?
Ans. That lumber was furnished to the Chesapeake and Ohio Canal Company, and was paid for by Mr. Sprigg, the Superintendent of the Cumberland Division of that Company. The bill and receipt are in my hand-writing?

Ques. Look at this bill and receipt for $400, (marked J. J. Bruce, $400,) purporting to be issued by you to Isaac F. Mans. State whether it is in your hand-writing, and whether the lumber receipted for was included in the bill and receipt for $1,257.10, which you have just looked at?
Ans. It is in my hand-writing, and was so included.

Ques. State whether any money was paid to you at the time you issued said receipt for $400?
Ans. No, sir. It was only a duplicate of part of the $1,257 10.

Ques. To whom was the receipt delivered?
Ans. To Mr. Alfred Spates.

Ques. At whose request?
Ans. At his request.

Ques. State, if you know it, for what purpose the receipt was issued?

Ans. Mr. Spates called upon me the day following the one on which I received payment for the $1,257.10 bill, and said he wished me to give him this bill for $400 of that amount of $1.257.10; he wanted a duplicate to present to the Board to show that a portion of that lumber went into a scow for the Georgetown Division; he did not want it to appear that the whole amount was used for the Cumberland Division.

Ques. How long have you lived in Allegany county?

Ans. I was born and raised in that county.

Ques. Do you know, or did you ever hear of any builder of boats in that county named Thomas Sheridan, except the foreman of Mr. Weld of that name?

Ans. No, sir; there is not, to my knowledge, any man of that name in Allegany county.

Ques. Would or would not your business necessarily make you acquainted with all the boat builders in that county?

Ans. I have transactions with all the boat builders in Cumberland, and have never heard of any one of that name except Mr. Weld's foreman.

Cross-Examination by Mr. Schley.

Ques. Please read the receipt of the bill marked Charge No. 3, J. J. Bruce, $1.257.10.

Ans. Received payment of R. M. Sprigg, Sup't. Signed by myself.

Ques. Will you be kind enough to read the receipt on that bill, (marked J. J. Bruce, $400?)

Ans. Received payment in full, Isaac R. Mans, Sup't., (signed,) J. J. Bruce.

Ques. In your dealings with the Canal Company do you not always specify in the receipt from whom you receive the money?

Ans. I never received money from any one but Sprigg, except on one occasion when I received some money from Mr. Spates.

Ques. Therefore whenever you gave Mr. Sprigg a receipt you always said, received from Richard M. Sprigg?

Ans. Yes, sir.

Ques. That $400 is included in the $1,257.10 receipt?

Ans. It is.

Ques. Please take the papers and show what part of the $1,257.10 bill applies to the $400 bill?

Ans. That is more than I can do, because I made the $400 bill according to Mr. Spates' dictation and direction. The $400 bill is not itemized. The lumber having been furnished just as it was ordered.

Ques. Was the receipt put there the same day the $400 bill was made out?

Ans. Yes, sir.

Ques. Did you not state in your examination in chief that the day after Mr. Sprigg paid you Mr. Spates called and asked for the $400 bill?

Ans. It may have been the same day, but my impression is it was the following day.

Ques. Look at the stamps on the two bills and state what are the dates on them?

Ans. It appears from that it was the same day.

Ques. Look at the $1,257.10 bill, and tell the Committee when the last charge was made on that bill?

Ans. On the 31st of October.

Ques. Look at the $400 bill and tell when the charge was made on that?

Ans. It is dated on the 9th of November, the same day Mr. Spates called.

Ques. Then the lumber was not sold on that day?

Ans. I dated it the 9th, just as Mr. Spates directed me he wanted the bill made out.

Ques. Was anybody with Mr. Spates at the time you made out the $400 bill?

Ans. No, sir; he came in my office alone.

Ques. Was or was not Richard Sprigg with him?

Ans. Not at the time the bill was made out.

Ques. Did or did not Mr. Spates pay you that $400 in the presence of Richard Sprigg?

Ans. He never paid me a cent of money in the presence of Mr. Sprigg.

Ques. Are you in the habit of giving duplicate receipts to different parties?

Ans. I am not.

Ques. But still you gave Mr. Spates a voucher for $400 which is included in the bill for $1,257.10?

Ans. I did it because he requested to do so. I supposed, as he was President of the Canal Company, he had a right to have what papers he wanted in connection with it.

Ques. Were you aware that you were giving receipts for $1,657.10 when you only received $1,257.10?

Ans. I did not look at it in that way. One of them is a duplicate for $400.

Ques. Your $100 receipt calls for two sides, sixty feet long. Now take the $1,257.10 receipt, and where is there any lumber sixty feet long?

Ans. Here is some 3687 feet of sixty feet siding.

Ques. Is any different sort of lumber used for gunneling and for the sides of boats?

Ans. I do not know anything about the construction of canal boats.

Ques. How long have you known Mr. Spates?

Ans. I suppose for twenty years.

Ques. Have you ever had any dealings with him?

Ans. I do not recollect of ever having any dealings with him until the last two or three years, when I furnished him some lumber.

Ques. Have you always been friendly?

Ans. Perfectly so.

Ques. You were a candidate against him last fall?

Ans. I was, sir.

Ques. In answer to a question, you stated you knew all the boat builders in Cumberland, and you knew no Tom Sheridan but the one on the stand yesterday. Might there not be another Tom Sheridan?

Ans. There might be a half dozen, but there is not another Tom Sheridan engaged in building boats in Cumberland.

Ques. Were you by the Company's boat yard in 1867.

Ans. I have been there frequently.

Ques. Did you see any ice breakers being built in that year?

Ans. I never paid any particular attention.

Ques. Might there not have been a Tom Sheridan building a boat there at that time without your knowing it?

Ans. N. J. Berston was their foreman at that time, and my orders came generally from him, sometimes from Mr. Sprigg.

By Mr. Clarke.

Ques. What lumber did you furnish to Mr. Spates?

Ans. I furnished him lumber on private account, plank and scantling for ordinary building.

Ques. Did you ever have any dishonest transactions with him?

Ans. Not to my knowledge. When these transactions were taking place I regarded Mr. Spates as a perfectly honest man. If I had had any reasons for supposing him dishonest, I would not have dealt with him in the way I did in regard to the voucher.

By Mr. Schley.

Ques. What is your opinion now of Mr. Spates?

Ans. Since the transactions have occurred, matters have transpired which have shaken my confidence in Mr. Spates' integrity.

Ques. What matters?

Ans. Matters in this investigation.

Ques. Then you believe the charges as made in the report of the Committee?

Ans. I believe them in regard to the transactions in which I am concerned.

Ques. Then you do not believe any other part of the report?

Ans. I do.

Ques. What are your political sentiments. Are you a Democrat or Republican?

Ans. I was a candidate of the Republican party, but the Republicans did not stick to me.

Ques. Were you not called on by Mr. Gordon and promised, if you would allow yourself to become a candidate, that he would support you and give you the benefit of his influence?

Ans. Mr. Gordon never approached me upon the subject prior to the nomination.

Ques. Were you not approached by R. D. Johnson in behalf of Mr. Gordon before the nomination?

Ans. No, sir; not in behalf of Mr. Gordon, or by anybody in behalf of Mr. Gordon.

Ques. After your nomination had you not an interview with Mr. Gordon in regard to the campaign?

Ans. I talked with Mr. Gordon on several occasions in regard to how the campaign was progressing.

Ques. Did he promise to support you?

Ans. He never directly promised, but I have every reason to think from his conversation he did.

Ques. Do you not know that Mr. Gordon was using his influence to secure your election?

Ans. I do not.

Ques. Look at that paper (marked J. H. Gordon, card No. 1) and state to the Committee whether or not you saw it circulated in Allegany county?

(Mr. Gordon stated that the paper referred to was a letter written by him to the Board of Public Works, and published by his permission.)

Ans. I have seen them circulated.

Ques. Did you circulate any of these papers in the county, and if so how many?

Ans. I may have handed a few of them to friends. Certainly not a half dozen passed out of my possession.

Ques. Look at that paper (marked J. H. Gordon's card, No. 2) and say whether you saw such a paper circulated in Allegany county prior to the nomination of Mr. Spates?

(Mr. Gordon stated that this paper was published by him in one of the papers of Cumberland.)

Ans. I saw that paper published subsequent to Mr. Spates' nomination.

Ques. Did you ever see that paper, or one like it, (marked card No. 3?)

Mr. Gordon—I furnished a copy of the resolutions of the Canal Company to Mr. Healey at his request, and he told me when he got them he intended to publish them, but I did not see the comments made upon them and did not know what they were until after the paper was published in that form.

Ans. I have seen one like it.

J. J. BRUCE.

TO THE PEOPLE OF ALLEGANY COUNTY.

By permission of J. H. Gordon, Esq., we present the following facts in regard to Alfred Spates, as forming *part* of the reasons which will induce us to repudiate him as a candidate for the State Senatorship.

MANY DEMOCRATS.

To the Honorable
  The Board of Public Works of Md.:

The following letter was forwarded to me by a member of the Board to whom it was addressed, and received on the 22d instant:

CUMBERLAND, Oct. 16, 1869.

Sir:—The object of this communication is to apprise you of the fact that J. H. Gordon, Esq., the President of the Canal Company, and William Devecmon, Esq., the Superintendent of the Division in this county, are using their influence, coupled with threats of dismissal of the employees of the Company, unless they will consent to vote against the nominees of the Democratic party in this county at the coming election.

As Chairman of the County Democratic Central Committee, I deem it my duty to apprise you of this state of affairs, and desire to know whether such a course, on the part of these officials, meets with your approval? If it does not, on behalf of the party, I make the request that you will at once take such steps in the matter as will prevent its occurrence. It is of the utmost importance, at this juncture, that the unity of the party in the county should be preserved.

Very respectfully, your obedient servant,

H. RESLEY,
Chairman Democratic Central Com., &c.

In reply, permit me to say that it is quite refreshing to see the new-born zeal which Mr. Resley shows for the preservation of the unity of the Democratic party.

He and his friend Spates did not think of the importance of this Democratic unity in June and July last, and from that time to the present, while they were denouncing and abusing the Democratic Board of Public Works for removing Spates from the Presidency of the Canal Company, on account of discoveries made in the books and papers of the Canal Company, by a gentleman appointed by the Board, unfavorable to the character of Spates for integrity. Nor did he think of the unity of the party when he and Spates, and other parties to the ring, were engaged, as they have been ever since June, in slandering and abusing me and the gentlemen of the Board of Directors, and interposing every possible difficulty in the way of our successful management of the affairs of the Canal Company.

But, so far as this abuse is concerned, I care but little for it. I have been abused by them before for trying to do my duty, and threatened with expulsion from the county because I would not agree with them in the efforts they were then making to destroy the Democratic party, and fasten upon the county the very policy which they now profess to oppose and abhor. I accepted the Presidency of the Canal Company with a determination to do my duty, and knowing that a performance of duty would bring me into collision with those men, I expected their abuse, and I should hardly feel that I deserved your confidence, or the confidence of the honest people of the State, if I was not abused by them.

As regards "threats of dismissal of the employees of the Company unless they will consent to vote against the nominees of the Democratic party in this county at the coming election," I can only say that I never made any such threats, or authorized them, but, on the contrary, I have uniformly told the men on the canal that the only condition that I would require of them, to retain their places, was prompt attention to their business and efficiency in the discharge of duty. I have also retained men in the employment of the Company, against the advice of many of my friends, who are openly engaged in personal abuse of you and myself, and active partisans of your enemies and mine.

Neither is it true that I am opposing the Democratic ticket, as you might infer from the letter, but I am opposing one man on that ticket, and I intend to oppose him whatever may be the consequences—I allude to Spates, the candidate for the Senate. I know that I hold my office of President of the Canal Company by your appointment, and that you have the power to remove me from that position, but I also know that I did not beg for the place; I took it with reluctance, and I shall not now beg to retain it.

When I was elected, I received the office with gratitude and as a high compliment, more on account of the manner in which it was given than on account of any benefit that I expected to derive from it. It was given, as you know, without condition, and I received it unpledged, except so far as every honest man, in taking an office, is pledged to the faithful performance of his duty.

I am glad to have the opportunity to explain my position and give the reasons for my course, and I think I shall stand justified in the opinion of every honest man in the State.

I will not support Spates, as a candidate for the Senate, for the following reasons:

After my election to the office of President of the Canal Company, he circulated the false statement, in this community, for the purpose of injuring both you and me, that I had received the office by making pledges to you that I would increase the tolls on the canal. This statement I pronounced a falsehood in the public papers of the county, and he made no reply to the charge. You know that Spates stated before the Board, at the election, that the tolls on coal could be increased to 52 cents per ton without injury to the canal.

The election of myself and the Board of Directors of the Canal Company, by you, imposed upon us, as you are aware, the duty of continuing the investigation into the accounts of the Company, which had been commenced by Mr. Wailes, under your direction. In the course of the investigation we found the following facts:

In 1866 the Canal Company condemned a right of way for a towing bridge across the mouth of Wills' Creek, passing over the lands of H. T. Weld and wife, for the use of the Rose Hill Wharf Company, with the understanding that the Wharf Company was to pay the cost of condemnation, and all expenses. Weld recovered a judgment for $725, at April term, 1866, and on the 21st September, 1866, J. Philip Roman, as attorney for the Canal Company, received from the Wharf Company the sum of $928.72, out of which he paid to me as attorney for Weld $739.62 on the same day, 21st September, 1866.

In March, 1868, the Canal Company placed in Spates' hand $10,000 to pay for condemnation of land at Cumberland, for a new basin, and in January, 1869, in accounting for this $10,000, he filed a copy of my receipt to Roman for the $739.62, but changed to bear date 21st September, 1868, and upon this, as a voucher, claimed and received a credit for the $739.62, as paid by him. On the 15th day of September, 1869, Mr. Gordon, as President of the Canal Company, called upon Spates for an explanation of this matter, and his explanation was given by a certificate of Mr. Moore, Cashier of the Second National Bank of Cumberland, that Spates had placed that sum to the credit of the Canal Company in the bank on that day.

It also appears that the city of Cumberland, in March, 1868, called upon the Canal Company to remove some old boats from the basin at Cumberland. The work was done in March, 1868, and reported to the Canal Company to have cost $1,682, as shown by the pay-roll for that month, and that sum was then paid by the Canal Company. In May, 1868. Mr. Spates called upon the city of Cumberland to pay part of that sum, under some arrangement with the Mayor, by which he claimed that the city was to pay part of it, and he then received a draft from the city for $540, payable four months after date, to him, as President of the Canal Company, which was paid in September, 1868, but Mr. Spates has never paid one cent of that money to the Canal Company, or in any manner accounted for it.

On the   day of October, 1869, Mr. Gordon wrote a note to Mr. Spates, which was handed to him by Mr. Wm. Devecmon, asking his explanation of this matter, but no explanation has been given, as yet.

The pay roll returned by the Superintendent of the Cumberland division of the Canal for July, 1868, shows that he paid to John J. Bruce the sum of $873.61 for lumber, and the receipt of Dr. Bruce for that sum is returned by the Superintendent as a voucher. Upon examining into the account of Dr. Bruce it is found to be made up in this way: Spates bought a bill of lumber from Dr. Bruce amounting to $576.20, out of which he built his carriage house and stable, which was charged to him by Dr. Bruce. This sum he, Spates, afterwards directed to be charged to the Canal Company, and stated at the time that he would settle with the Company for it. Spates was then credited with the amount, and it was charged to the Canal Company, and this sum with the sum of $297.41, for lumber bought by the Company, made up the sum of $873.61 paid to Bruce by the Company. The sum of $68.74 for lumber bought by Spates, was charged to the Canal Company in September, 1868, in the same manner, and reported by the Superintendent and paid in the same manner, but neither of these sums has yet been accounted for by Spates or paid to the Canal Company.

The pay rolls of the Canal Company, returned by Sprigg for the Cumberland Division, show that Nicholas Furlong was returned as a laborer in the employment of the Company for the whole twelve months of the year 1868, at one dollar and fifty cents per day; but no such man can be found to have been in the Company's service during that time. But there is a Nicholas Furlong, who is a special friend of Spates, and a watchman in the Second National Bank of Cumberland, which occupies part of Spates' property, and who was paid for his services in the manner above stated.

Now, gentlemen, if I am expected to vote for Spates, in the face of these, I can only say that I am disappointed in the object for which you appointed me; and I cannot consent to that species of self degradation. But I know that you had your own suspicions of his want of integrity, and that he was removed on that account; and I know that

I will be sustained by you in the course I have pursued, in turning out and exposing his frauds, and I shall also be sustained by you and the honest people of the State generally, in refusing to vote for him or giving him any kind of support for a place in which he, owing to the corrupt manner in which he has conducted the business heretofore entrusted to him, would only become more dangerous.

If he was unworthy of your confidence and could not receive your votes for a place of trust, upon the report of Mr. Wailes, you surely cannot expect me to support him after the additional facts above stated have been shown.

There are many other matters of a similar character which I might state if it was necessary, but I will not detain you longer with these disgusting details. And now, in conclusion,

I remain, very sincerely and truly,

Yours, &c.,

J. H. GORDON.

At a meeting of the Board of President and Directors of the Chesapeake and Ohio Canal, held at their office in Washington city, D. C., on the 11th day of March, 1868, the following order was passed:

Ordered that ten thousand dollars ($10,000) be advanced to the President, to be applied to the cost and expense attending the condemnation of land at Cumberland, Md., required for the extension of the canal and basin at that place.

I certify that the above is a true and exact copy from the journal of proceedings of that date.

BENJ. FAWCETT,

Clerk.

List of condemnations returned by *Alfred Spates, President of the Chesapeake and Ohio Canal, on the 7th of January,* 1869, *and referred by the Board to the Committee on Accounts.*

1 Thomas I. and R. S. McKaig.	$1,400 00
2 Thomas I McKaig, (Trustee)	5,000 00
3 H. Willison, Sheriff's bill	409 30
4 Jacob Earlougher	850 00
5 T. I. McKaig, A. Beall, W. W. McKaig, and others	1,000 00
6 Thomas I. McKaig, (Trustee)	1,000 00
7 H. Resley, Clerk	72 25
8 Patrick Murray, Judgments	324 00
9 Thomas H. Weld and wife	739 62
10 D. Duncan, (late Sheriff,) on account of H. T. Weld and wife	55 60
	$10,850 77
Amount placed in his hands March 11, 1868	10,000 00
Balance paid Spates, February 4th, 1869	850 77

No money has ever been accounted for at this office on account of the Rose Hill Wharf Company.

The Weld case stands as follows:

Condemnation, &c...$739 62
D. Duncan, Sheriff's fees.. 55 60

$795 22

I certify that the above is a true copy from the papers filed in this office.

BENJ. FAWCETT.
Clerk and Treas. Ches. and Ohio Canal.

Ches. & Ohio Canal Co. } In the Circuit Court for
vs } Allegany County.
H. Thomas Weld and Emily Weld. } No. 163.

Trials, April Term, 1868. Inquisition, 1868, April 8. Objection of Deft. May 18. Affdt. of H. T. Weld for continuance, motion for same, motion for continuance overruled, Inquisition affirmed for $872 and costs.

1868, Dec. 9th. Satisfied per receipt filed. The receipt is dated 21st Sept., 1868.

Received Sept. 21st, 1868, of J. Philip Roman for the Chesapeake and Ohio Canal Company, the sum of seven hundred and thirty-nine dollars and sixty-two cents on account of the above case.

J. H. GORDON,
Att'y for Weld and Wife.

State of Maryland, Allegany County, to wit:

I, Horace Resley, Clerk of the Circuit Court for Allegany County, do hereby certify the above and foregoing to be truly taken from the record and proceedings of the Court.

HORACE RESLEY,
Clerk C. C. for Allegany County.

Rose Hill Wharf Co. to Ches. and Ohio Co., Dr.

To cash paid H. T. Weld and wife, condemnation.............$725 00
Interest from May 24, 1866, to September 21..................... 14 62
Stamp.. 50
Warrant.. 50
Sheriff's fees and Jurors... 58 90
Clerk's costs and recording.. 27 20
J. Philip Roman, attorney... 100 00

$926 72
Costs of injunction.. 2 00

$928 72

Received of James M. Schley, attorney, nine hundred and twenty-eight dollars and twenty-two cents, in full of the above till errors be corrected.

J. PHILIP ROMAN,
Attorney for Ches. and Ohio Canal Co.
Cumberland, Sept. 21, 1866.

CUMBERLAND, Sept. 14th, 1869.
MR. ALFRED SPATES,

Sir:—It appears by the books and proceedings of the Chesapeake and Ohio Canal Company, that the sum of ten thousand dollars was placed by that Company in your hands, while you were its President, for the purpose of paying for condemnation of land at Cumberland; and it also appears that in settling with the Canal Company for that sum of five thousand dollars you claimed and received credit for the sum of seven hundred and thirty-nine dollars, paid by J. Philip Roman, for the Canal Company, to Josiah H. Gordon, as attorney for Henry Thos. Weld and wife, for condemnation in No. 163 trials, to April term, 1868, in the Circuit Court for Allegany county, being for $725.00 damages and costs in the case of Weld and wife, for the right of way for the towing bridge of the Rose Hill Wharf Company, over the mouth of Wills' Creek.

It also appears by a receipt of J. Philip Roman, as attorney for the Canal Company, to the Rose Hill Wharf Company, that Mr. Roman received said sum of money from the Wharf Company, and that it has therefore been paid by the Canal Company and the Wharf Company both, or else you have claimed and received a credit for that amount of money from the Canal Company which you did not pay, and have no right to.

I would be glad to have your explanation of this matter at once, as I am required to make a report to the Committee of Accounts of the Canal Company, which is now waiting my reply.

Yours, etc.,

J. H. GORDON,
President Ches. and Ohio Canal Co.

Second National Bank, Cumberland, Md., Sept. 15, 1869. Benj. Fawcett, C. and Treas· Chesapeake and Ohio Canal Co., Annapolis, Md.

Dear Sir:—Col. A. Spates has this day placed to the credit of your Company $739.

Very respct. yours,

EDWIN L. MOORE.

Owing to the desperate efforts that are now being made to prejudice this community against myself and the Board of Directors of the Canal Company, and to persuade the people that Mr. Spates has been a very much persecuted man because he was not permitted to hold the office of President during his natural life, I now publish the above documents without comment.

The Board will shortly be able to lay before the people of the State a full report of the condition of the Canal and its accounts and general affairs that will be its best vindication from all slanders.

J. H. GORDON.

TO THE PEOPLE OF ALLEGANY COUNTY.

The reply of Mr. SPATES to the statements of Mr. GORDON has been published. It is worthless, and disproves none of the charges made against him by Mr. GORDON, but in fact *admits them to be true by the very manner in which he has tried to cover up and excuse his actions.* But in order that none may be humbugged as to his character, and to show that Mr. Gordon's estimate of him is true, the following *official record* is placed before you as additional evidence of corruption on the part of Mr. Spates:

OFFICE CHESAPEAKE AND OHIO CANAL COMPANY,
WASHINGTON CITY, October 9th, 1869.

At a meeting of the President and Directors of this Company, held in the City of Washington, on Thursday, August 9th, 1866, the following preamble and resolutions were adopted:

WHEREAS, Congress, by an Act approved March 3d, 1863, making appropriations for sundry civil expenses of the Government for the year ending June 30th, 1864, (see section 21,) appropriated the sum of $13,000 for the purpose of raising and reconstructing certain bridges over the Canal, in Georgetown, D. C., which sum was to be expended under the direction of the Chesapeake and Ohio Canal Company;

AND WHEREAS, The Company have been prevented, until the 26th of June and 6th of July last, from making these desirable and needed improvements for want of consent of the corporation of Georgetown, which consent is now given;

AND WHEREAS, Upon application of the Treasurer of this Company at the Treasury Department, we are, *for the first time,* informed that said sum of $13,000 was drawn from the Treasury of the United States on or about the 11th of February, 1865, by Alfred Spates, late President of the Company:

Therefore be it resolved, That the said Alfred Spates be at once called upon, by the Treasurer of the Company, to return the said sum of $13,000 into the United States Treasury, or place it so that it may be at once available for the purposes indicated by the appropriation.

Resolved, That upon the failure of the Treasurer of this Company to accomplish the objects of the aforegoing resolutions, by the 1st of September next, he be and is hereby instructed to report the fact to the proper officers of the United States Treasury Department, that the necessary proceedings be instituted by the Department for the recovery of the said $13,000.

" I certify that the above is a true copy from the Journal of Proceedings of that date.

BENJAMIN FAWCETT,
Clerk and Treasurer Chesapeake and Ohio Canal Co.

I certify that from the books of the Company it appears that the above mentioned $13,000 was deposited to the credit of the Company on the 19th of September, 1866.

BENJAMIN FAWCETT,
Clerk and Treasurer.

The above speaks for itself, and shows a bold attempt by Spates to defraud the Canal Company out of $13,000, which he held and used for his own benefit for one year, seven months and eight days—part of which time he was out of the Presidency—and that he never gave it up until the Canal Company found it out and *compelled him* to return it, and even then he did not and never has accounted for the interest upon it, which amounts to $1,252.33.

After Mr. Spates was turned out and Mr. Gordon appointed to the Presidency of the Canal Company, Mr. Spates stated that Mr. Gordon had gotten the Presidency by pledging to the Board that he would raise the tolls on the Canal. Mr. Gordon published a card in the *Alleganian,* pronouncing Mr. Spates a liar. Mr. Spates has never to this day denied that he is one. What were the real facts about the offer to raise the tolls? They are these: *Mr. Spates, himself,* offered to the Board of Public Works, a calculation showing that the tolls could be safely raised to 52 cents per ton on coal, and *endeavored to have them raised.*

The above facts have been furnished by Mr Gordon; the resolutions are a matter of *record;* and any one who doubts the latter statement, as to the tolls, can see the calculations, *in the handwriting of Mr Spates himself,* at the office of Mr. Gordon.

What shall the honest Democracy of Allegany say to *such a man on* Tuesday next!

47

TUESDAY, March 8th, 1870.

BENJAMIN FAWCETT sworn.

By Mr. Poe.

Ques. Please look at the estimate of Mr. Mans, for the Georgetown Division, and state whether the words "For Scow and Transportation, $450," were inserted by you, and, if so, by whose direction?

Ans. I inserted them by direction of the President.

Ques. How much money was paid to Mr. Mans on that estimate?
Ans. $2,950.

Ques. Is the endorsement on the estimate in your handwriting?
Ans. It is.

BENJ. FAWCETT.

CHARGE No. 2.

MONDAY, March 7th, 1870.

The Committee met at 7½ o'clock, P. M., pursuant to adjournment.

Present—Messrs. Henry, (Chairman,) Sellman and Clarke; also Messrs. Spates, Schley and Gordon.

JOHN SHAY was called and sworn.

By Mr. Gordon.

Ques. Were you the Superintendent of the Antietam Division of the Chesapeake and Ohio Canal in October and November, 1868?

Ans. I was.

Ques. Did you furnish an estimate of money to be expended upon your Division in October of that year?

Ans. I did.

Ques. Look at that paper, (marked John Shay, No. 1,) and state whether that is the paper?

Ans. If that is the one I sent to the Canal Board, it is the paper.

Ques. Is the signature to that paper in your handwriting?

Ans. I think it is my clerk's.

Ques. In whose handwriting are the words "Scow, lumber, paddle and frames, $1,000," on that paper?

Ans. I do not know.

Ques. Had you made out that bill for $2,465.83 or for $1,465.83?

Ans. For $1,465.83, which were the actual expenses of the Division.

Ques. State what you know about it?

Ans. There was a thousand dollars added to the $1,465.83 for a scow, or ice breaker, some lumber, paddles and frames, &c.

Ques. By whose direction was that thousand dollars added?

Ans. By the direction of Mr. Spates and Mr. Fawcett.

Ques. Look at that paper now shown to you, (marked J. J. Bruce's Receipt for $652.60,) and state whether you know anything about it?

Ans. If that is the one I returned to the Canal Company's office, as a matter of course I got it from Mr. Spates at Cumberland.

Ques. Have you one like it, and, if so, produce it?

Ans. I have one like it which I file, (marked Duplicate of J. J. Bruce's Receipt for $652.60.)

Ques. Do you keep duplicates of your bills, and, if so, why?

Ans. I do; I send one to office, and hold the other myself.

Ques. What did you do with the $2,465.83, the amount of the check?

Ans. I endorsed the check, and Mr. Spates took it to Cumberland and sent me the amount of money that was due for my Division, something less than $1,500.

Ques. What became of the balance?

Ans. He sent me vouchers for the balance of the money. The paper presented by me (marked Duplicate of J. J. Bruce's Receipt for $652.60) was one of them.

Ques. Is the paper marked (Receipt of Hills, Gephart & Co., for $349.96.) one of them?

Ans. It is. I file a duplicate, marked (Duplicate of Receipt of Hills, Gephart & Co., for $349.96.)

Ques. Are the papers marked (Receipt of John Tauber for $22.00,) and (Receipt of Jacob Brengle for $12.13,) two of those vouchers?

Ans. They are; I also file duplicates of those papers.

Ques. Were those the vouchers which made up the difference between the sum of money sent you and the check which you received?

Ans. Those are the vouchers.

Cross-Examination by Mr. Schley.

Ques. Did you receive the scows, lumber, paddles and frames?

Ans. I did; I think all that those bills call for are there.

Ques. Do you use it as a scow in the summer and an ice breaker in the winter?

Ans. We do.

Ques. Did you request Mr. Spates to get the scow, lumber, paddles and frames for you, and, if so, why?

Ans. I requested him to get them because he was in Cumberland and I was only half way there, and because he could get them done better than I could in any other place, and because they were always furnished from Cumberland.

By Mr. Gordon.

Ques. Look at that paper, marked (Abstract of John Shay for October, 1868,) and state whether that is your abstract?

Ans. I think that is it.

Ques. Look over the list of bills entered there, and state whether you made those entries from the bills themselves?

Ans. I did, and returned the bills, with the abstract, to the office.

Ques. Look at the entry, "check $2500." Is that the amount of the check you received?

Ans. Yes, sir.

Ques. You received something more than your estimate called for, then?

Ans. I did.

(Mr. Schley offered in evidence the endorsement on the abstract "Examined and approved February 1st, 1869. (Signed) John P. Thomas and Esau Pickerell, Committee on Accounts.")

JOHN SHAY.

Dr. John J. Bruce recalled.

By Mr. Gordon.

Ques. Look at the papers (marked J. J. Bruce's receipt, $652.60, and duplicate receipt of J. J. Bruce, $652.60,) and state what you know of them?

Ans. Those are my bills and receipts, in my hand-writing.

Ques. To whom did you give those papers?

Ans. To Mr. Spates.

Ques. Did Mr. Spates give you any money on those bills, and if so, how much?

Ans. He paid me on those bills $252.60.

Ques. Who paid you the balance?

Ans. The $400 was the amount Mr. Sprigg paid me. That portion of the bill was a duplicate of a part of the bill for the Cumberland Division of $1,267.10

Ques. Is that the bill and receipt to which you refer, (paper marked Charge No. 3, J. J. Bruce, $1,257.10?)

Ans. Yes, sir. The $400 there represents the $400 of that amount.

Ques. Did you ever furnish any lumber to Mr. Shay at all?

Ans. I furnished the $252.60 of that bill upon the order of Mr. Shay.

Cross-examination by Mr. Schley.

Ques. Look at the $1,257.10 bill, and state on what day the last charge was made?

Ans. On the 31st of October.

Ques. Look on the $400 bill, and state on what day the last charge was made on that?

Ans. On November 9th.

Ques. If you dated the last bill November 9th, why did you date the other bill October 31st?

Ans. That was the date on which the lumber was furnished. When Mr. Spates came to pay the $252.60, he requested me to add $400 to the bill, because the lumber was furnished for an ice breaker.

Ques. Then you gave duplicates for $2,057.10 when you received only $1,257.10?

Ans. I did.

Ques. Then the lumber was not bought on November 9th?

Ans. No, sir; I dated it at Mr. Spates' request.

Ques. What time in the day did Mr. Sprigg call and pay you the $1,257.10 bill?

Ans. I cannot recollect.

Ques. You say Mr. Spates paid you $252.60 but did not pay you the $400.

Ans. Yes, sir.

Ques. Was anybody with Mr. Spates when he paid you the Shay bill?

Ans. No, sir.

Ques. Was or was not Richard Sprigg with him?

Ans. No, sir.

Ques. Did or did not Mr. Spates, in the presence of Mr. Sprigg, between three and four o'clock on the 9th day of November, come into your office, and Mr. Spates put his hand into his pantaloons pocket and drew out a large roll of money and paid you the Mans and the Shay bills in the presence of Mr. Sprigg?

Ans. No, sir. The only amount he paid me was the $252.60, and there was no person in the office at the time.

Ques. Did or did not Mr. Sprigg as Superintendent of the Cumberland Division caution you time and again never to charge in his bill lumber for any other Division?

Ans. No, sir. The lumber worked in the shops at Cumberland for other Divisions he directed to be charged in his bill.

Ques. Did or did you not at various times get the accounts mixed, charging to the Cumberland Division lumber for other Divisions, and did not Mr. Sprigg direct your attention to it, and had he not some trouble in correcting it?

Ans. He directed me to keep the lumber as far as I could separate, but it was all charged in his bill, and he always paid for it; it made no difference what the lumber was used for—whether for his Division or not.

Re-Examination by Mr. Gordon.

Ques. Look at those papers (marked J. J. Bruce $652.60 and duplicate) and state whether they are duplicates?

Ans. They are.

Ques. Did you know anything of an order of the Board under which those ice breakers were built?

Ans. No, sir?

Ques. Did Mr. Spates ask you to put that on?

Ans. Yes, sir. That portion of the bill was made just as he directed.

Ques. Did you know any order of the Board for the building of Mans' boat?.

Ans. No, sir.

Ques. Did you require a special order of the Board to furnish lumber?

Ans. No, sir.

Ques. Upon whose order did you generally furnish lumber?

Ans. Generally upon the order of the foreman, Mr. Berston, sometimes on the order of Mr. Sprigg himself.

Ques. He did not tell you that the Board had passed an order for him to come and get the lumber?

Ans. No, sir.

Re-Cross-Examination by Mr. Schley.

Ques. How came you to charge for hauling on the $652.60 bill.

Ans. We always charge for hauling.

Ques. Look at the $1,200 bill and see if there is any charge for hauling on it?

Ans. Yes, sir; in every case.

J. J. BRUCE.

TUESDAY, March 8th, 1870.

BENJAMIN FAWCETT sworn.

By Mr. Poe.

Ques. Look at the estimate of Mr. Shay and state if the words " scow, lumber, paddle and frames, $1,000" are in your handwriting, and if so, by whose direction they were added?

Ans. They were added by me by direction of the President.

Ques. How much was paid to Mr. Shay under that estimate?
Ans. Twenty-five hundred dollars.

Ques. Was the endorsement on that estimate made by you?
Ans. It was.

CHARGE No. 4.

TUESDAY, March 8th, 1870.

The Committee met at 9½ o'clock A. M., pursuant to adjournment.

Present—Messrs. Henry, Chairman, Clarke and Sellman; also Messrs. Spates, Schley, Gordon and Poe.

BENJAMIN FAWCETT sworn.

By Mr. Poe.

Ques. How long have you been clerk and treasurer of the Chesapeake and Ohio Canal Company?

Ans. I went into office on the 1st of May, 1868.

Ques. Was it your duty as clerk and treasurer to make the monthly payments to the Superintendents of the various Divisions?

Ans. It was my duty to draw the checks and countersign them.

Ques. Look at the estimate of George W. Spates for the month of October, 1868, now shown you, and state whether that estimate was presented by George W. Spates, and when?

(Marked estimate of George W. Spates for October, 1868.)

Ans. It was presented by George W. Spates on the fifth of November 1868.

Ques. State whether you paid to him any money under that estimate, when, and how much, and produce the check with his endorsement, if you have it?

Ans. I paid him $3,100 on that estimate, and produce the check, (marked George W. Spates' check for $3,100.)

Ques. Look at the abstract or statement of expenditures of the Seneca Division, No. 4, now shown to you, and state whether that abstract was returned by George W. Spates, and is in his handwriting?

Ans. It is all in his handwriting with the exception of the two last items on the third page.

Ques. Look at the list of bills paid, as set down in that abstract, and state whether H. P. Tasker & Co, $1,200, and H. P. Tasker & Co., $150, are in the handwriting of George W. Spates?

Ans. From my knowledge of his handwriting, I think they are.

Ques. Look at the bills and receipts of H. P. Tasker & Co., one dated November 9th, 1868, for $1,200, and one dated November 18th, 1868, for $150, signed H. P. Tasker & Co., (marked H. P. Tasker & Co.'s receipts for $1,200 and $150) and state whether they are the bills and receipts which were filed by George W. Spates among his vouchers for payments to those amounts with his said abstract?

Ans. Those are the two bills filed by him.

Ques. Whose memorandum is "voucher No. 54"?

Ans. Mr. Peck, the assistant bookkeeper in the Canal office.

Ques. State whether you examined the two bills of which you have just spoken, and receipts, at the time they were returned to the office or shortly after, and whether you identify them as the same?

Ans. I did examine them, and do identify them as the same.

Cross-Examination by Mr. Schley.

Ques. At the time these papers were returned to the office, who was the clerk?

Ans. I was.

Ques. What position had Mr. Peck?

Ans. Assistant clerk.

Ques. When these abstracts come into the office do you take possession of them?

Ans. They are all addressed to me, and I generally open them and hand them to Mr. Peck, the assistant clerk, who has particular charge of that branch of the business.

Ques. Do you recollect whether you opened this particular one of George W. Spates?

Ans. I cannot say positively whether I did or not, but I always open them when there, and I was rarely away.

Ques. Then you say you did open it?

Ans. I am satisfied I opened it.

Ques. How came your attention to be particularly directed to this abstract of George W. Spates?

Ans. I am in the habit of going over the vouchers and abstracts, and did it in this particular case because I had doubts about the genuineness of the vouchers.

Ques. What gave rise to those suspicions?

Ans. I had been led to believe from Mr. Sprigg's estimates and from what I had heard said in the Board, that those boats had been built at Cumberland at the expense of the Cumberland Division.

Ques. Did you put any particular mark on those papers by which you could identify them as the ones you handed over to Mr. Peck?

Ans. No, sir.

Ques. Did you take those particular abstracts out of the bundles and put them away anywhere?

Ans. They remained in the office with the other papers, and were not filed away until after they were examined by the Committee, which was afterwards done.

Ques. When did you next see those papers?

Ans. I cannot name any particular time.

Ques. Do you recollect of having looked at them again until the new Board came in?

Ans. Yes, sir, several times. I looked at them, at the instance of Judge Bowie, who asked me to send him a statement of them in December, 1868.

Ques. Have these papers been out of the office?

Ans. They have been out of the office in charge of the Committee.

Ques. Were they out of the office before the Committee took them?

Ans. No, sir.

Ques. Did you ever show them to anybody in the city of Washington?

Ans. I think not.

Ques. Did you ever show them to a gentleman named Kilgour, or tell him the contents of the papers, or that you had reason to think those two papers were forgeries?

Ans. I never talked to Kilgour until after the Committee reported to the Board, and then gave him no definite information in regard to the matter, although he frequently tried to get at the information.

Ques. Did Mr. Wales ever have these papers out of the office?

Ans. I think not. Mr. Wales examined them in the office.

Ques. When these persons were examining these papers, before the Committee commenced its investigation, were you present the whole time they were looking at them?

Ans. Yes, sir. Nobody examined them, to my knowledge, except the parties entitled to examine them.

Ques. Have you ever talked to anybody else in regard to these matters?

Ans. I have talked to various persons who called to see me, but have refrained from communicating anything to them. Mr. Watkins frequently applied to me for information, and I showed him the report of the Committee.

Ques. When did the conversation with Mr. Kilgour take place?

Ans. I do not know. I used to see him nearly every day.

Ques. Where was this report made to the Board?

Ans. At Annapolis?

Ques. Where did you have the conversation with Mr. Kilgour?

Ans. In Washington city.

Ques. Was the conversation prior to or subsequent to the report?

Ans. I do not know.

Ques. Did anybody know of the report except the President and Directors, and those in the office, prior to the time the report was made to the stockholders' meeting?

Ans. It was generally known that an examination was going on, and that a report would be made.

Ques. Did you ever go to anybody and tell them that a report was made?

Ans. I think not.

Ques. Would you be able to identify all the vouchers filed, with the various abstracts, since you have been in the office?

Ans. No, sir.

Ques. And still you undertake to identify those two papers?

Ans. I do. My attention was particularly called to the papers connected with this transaction.

Ques. Have the Committee on Accounts had those papers?

Ans. They had them while making the examination at Cumberland. After they got through, the papers were returned to me, and I kept them under lock and key in the safe.

Ques. Was there an excursion of the President and Directors of the canal to Georgetown?

Ans. There was.

Ques. Were you along, and did you have the papers with you?
Ans. I was, and had the papers with me in my satchel.

Ques. Where did you keep your satchel?
Ans. In the state-room.

Ques. Did you have your eye on it all the time?
Ans. I did not, but kept it under lock and key.

Ques. What did you do with them when you got to Georgetown?
Ans. I carried them to Washington and locked them up. I kept them there until such time as the Committee called for them.

Ques. Did you take them to Cumberland after that trip?
Ans. I did not.

Ques. Afterwards you were summoned before the grand jury?
Ans. I was.

Ques. Did you take the papers with you?
Ans. I did, but did not go before the grand jury, because it was not in session.

Ques. What did you do with the papers then?
Ans. I brought them back with me.

Ques. Where did you stop in Cumberland?
Ans. At the Barnum house.

Ques. How did you take the papers?
Ans. In my satchel. When I got to the Barnum house I locked them up in the room I slept in. When I went to the court house I left the papers in charge of Mr. Mans and Mr. Mulvaney.

Ques. When these estimates are made by the Division Superintendents are they not laid before the Board and approved by them?
Ans. Yes, sir.

Ques. Was there an entry made of such approval in the journal of proceedings, and, if so, produce the book?
Ans. There was such an entry made, and I produce the book.

(Mr. Schley offered in evidence the statement on page 119, Proceedings for Nov. 6, 1868, that the estimate for October of Geo. W. Spates, amounting to $3100, was laid before the Board, approved, and the Treasurer ordered to draw check for the same, to show that it was not the act of Mr. Spates, but was approved by the Board.)

Ques. Prior to the meeting of the Board of Public Works in June, 1869, had you or not a conversation with Mr. Peck, and in that conversation did you or not say that it was a fight between you and Col. Spates, and one or the other of you had to go out?
Ans. I cannot say whether I had such a conversation or not, but I entertained that view of the case from what I had heard from others, not from anything that had occurred between Mr. Spates and myself.

Ques. Had not you and Mr. Spates always been friends up to that time?

Ans. No, sir; Mr. Spates never was a friend of mine.

Ques. Were you a friend of his?

Ans. As much so as I was to any man with whom I never had any intercourse. I always regarded Mr. Spates as very much opposed to my getting the position.

Ques. Do you know whether or not Mr. Spates voted for your appointment?

Ans. I do not think there was a vote taken.

Ques. Did you or not, at a camp-meeting in Montgomery, circulate some of those circulars put out by Mr. Gordon?

Ans. No, sir.

Ques. Did you ever give any of them to anybody to circulate?

Ans. No, sir.

Ques. Did you, at a camp-meeting in Montgomery county, meet with Isaac Young, and hand one of these circulars to him?

Ans. I was at the camp-meeting in Montgomery, and staid with Isaac Young, but I never had but one of Mr. Gordon's circulars at all, and have no knowledge of giving it to him, or having any conversation with him on the subject. I have no recollection of having had the circular with me.

By Mr. Clarke.

Ques. By whom were you appointed to your office?

Ans. I was appointed by a resolution offered by Judge Bowie.

Re-Examination by Mr. Poe.

The President does not vote, except in case of a tie, by the provisions of the charter?

Ans. No.

Ques. The coolness grew up between you and Mr. Spates whilst you were in the Board together?

Ans. Not upon my part. Mr. Spates did not treat me in the way I thought I was entitled to be treated, and whilst the examination was going on I had reason to think that parties were employed to watch my conduct and report what transpired.

Ques. Did not the coolness grow out of your examination into the accounts?

Ans. I thought so.

Ques. Did not some of the members of the Board participate in your opinions?

Ans. Judge Bowie looked into the accounts in connection with me.

Ques. How came Mr. Wales to examine into the accounts of the Canal Company?

Ans. Mr. Wales was appointed by the Board of Public Works to investigate and examine the books and accounts of the Canal Company by a resolution passed May 7, 1869, entered on page 159 of the proceedings of the President and Directors of the Canal Company as follows:

"On motion, it was unanimously ordered that the Clerk and "Treasurer afford every facility asked or required to enable a thorough "and full investigation of all books and accounts of said Company "either at the city of Annapolis or elsewhere, and the Board further "expresses its willingness to grant or furnish any additional facilities "or information that may be required, and that the clerk furnish a copy "of the above resolution to Mr. Wales, and the members of the Board "of Public Works of Maryland."

By Mr. Schley.

Ques. Who offered that resolution?

Ans. The President drew the resolution himself for this investigation.

By Mr. Poe.

Ques. Did not Wales make a report on Nov. 5th?

Ans. I understood he did.

BENJ. FAWCETT.

H. P. TASKER sworn.

By Mr. Poe.

Ques. Where did you live in November, 1868, and what was your business?

Ans. I was living in Cumberland. My business was general groceries, provision, coal and lumber business.

Ques. Where was your place of business?

Ans. At the head of Baltimore street, immediately on the railroad.

Ques. Look at the two accounts now shown you, (marked receipt of H. P. Tasker & Co. for $1,200, and receipt of H. P. Tasker & Co. for $150) and state whether the writing or any part of it, or the signature, is in your hand or in the hand of any person in your employ or connected with you in business?

Ans. No part of the writing is in my hand or in the hand of any person in my employ.

Ques. Are not those bills made out on your ordinary printed form?

Ans. Yes. The billheads are genuine.

Ques. State to the Committee whether you, or anybody concerned for you, ever sold the lumber mentioned in those bills to the Chesapeake and Ohio Canal Company, or any of its agents or Superintendents?

Ans. All the lumber we have sold to the Canal Company was entered on the books, amounting in the aggregate to $293.17.

Ques. Look at that bill, (marked H. P. Tasker & Co.'s receipt for $293.17) and see whether that bill represents the transaction?

Ans. This is the true statement made out by Mr. McCulley, receipted for on the ninth of November, 1868.

Ques. Is that the only transaction your house has ever had with the Canal Company?

Ans. It is, except that we sold them some rope—bow lines and tow lines—less than a hundred dollars' worth.

Ques. Do you think that at the time that bill was settled you gave those billheads to Mr. Spates?

Ans. Mr. Spates, when he came to pay the bill, made some objection to its form, and said that the material was intended for two separate purposes. Mr. McCulley said he did not know how to divide the bill, and Mr. Sprigg and Mr. Spates said they could fix it themselves, and I gave them two billheads. That is my recollection.

Ques. These two bills for $1,200 and $150 were not executed by any one in your firm, the articles not bought, and the money not received?

Ans. No, sir.

Ques. Look at the cancelled stamps and see whether the writing is different from the other?

Ans. The handwriting was evidently not done by any one in our concern.

Ques. Had you ever any transaction with George W. Spates?

Ans. No, sir. I do not think I ever saw him until yesterday evening, and have had no communication with him by letter.

Ques. Do you know anything of orders of the Canal Board for lumber for building an ice breaker or house boat.

Ans. I do not.

Ques. Who gave the order for the $293.17 bill?

Ans. Mr. Berston, I think.

Cross-Examination by Mr. Schley.

Ques. You said, in answer to the first question, your place of business was at the head of Baltimore street; had you any other place of business?

Ans. No, sir, except the office at the lumber yard, and after I turned the lumber yard over to the firm on the 16th of July, I never transacted any business there.

Ques. Who paid you the $293.17 bill?

Ans. The money was paid to Mr. McCulley. Mr. Sprigg and Mr. Spates came in together. I think Mr. Sprigg paid it, but am not certain.

Ques. Did not I understand you to say, in your testimony in chief, that Mr. Spates paid the bill?

Ans. It was paid by his order. I do not know whether he counted out the money or not.

Ques. When you went into the firm with Slack & Co., the lumber yard was independent of that?

Ans. That was my own individual business up to that time. I put that in as so much capital stock.

Ques. Where did you get the lumber from?

Ans. From four or five different mills. The principal part of it came from my brother's mill at Altamont.

Ques. How was the $293.17 delivered to the Canal Company?

Ans. The two first items came from the lumber yard. The other portion was sawed to order and delivered on a pair of trucks. It did not come into the yard. That was the only lumber on cars the Canal Company ever got from me.

Ques. Was Ezekiel Male in your employment?

Ans. He was. He employed men and unloaded the trucks.

Ques. Did you see it delivered?

Ans. I did not. I trusted all that business to Mr. Male.

Ques. Do you not recollect being with Male when the car load of lumber for the canal was unloaded, and saying to him if you could get many such contracts like that you would be all right?

Ans. No, sir. I am not in the habit of speaking of my business in that way, to employees especially.

Ques. Show on that bill which of the lumber came from your brother's mill and which from other mills?

Ans. All the last charges came from my brother's mill.

Ques. Did you get any lumber for the Canal Company from Oakland or Offert's mill?

Ans. No.

Ques. When did you go into a partnership with the firm?

Ans. I think on the 16th of July.

Ques. How long did you stay in the firm?

Ans. Until about the 5th or 6th of February, 1869.

Ques. When you dissolved did you take stock and ascertain the share each one had in the firm?

Ans. The books were balanced on the 1st of January, from that time we lumped it. I got the present worth of my stock and claiming consideration for having established the business and the right to remain in it for a year. I got $500 for going out.

Ques. Did you get anything else?

Ans. They paid me back the amount of my stock as credited on the books.

Ques. Was or was not, in your settlement with the firm, your lumber account short?

Ans. No, sir; it was not.

Ques. Then there was not a charge that more lumber went out than was accounted for?

Ans. There was a charge to that effect but it was a mistake.

Ques. Was it ever looked into and rectified?

Ans. It was. After I left, Mr. Slack made an estimate of the amount of lumber that had been received and approximated the number of feet that had been sold and struck a balance. The men authorized measured only that which suited them and some of it was never measured, and much of it was split up and nothing allowed for shrinkage. I afterwards had another measurement when it overran.

Ques. Did I understand you to say you gave Col. Spates those billheads?

Ans. That is my recollection. He wanted it in two separate bills. Mr. McCulley and I did not know how to divide it. Berston I thought ought to be the man to do it, I was very glad to get rid of it, but expected him to bring them back to be signed. I gave them to Mr. Spates individually.

Ques. Richard M. Sprigg was there all the time was he?

Ans. Yes. I think they went out together.

Ques. Did all this conversation pass between you and Mr. Spates in reference to the $293.17 bill?

Ans. Yes, sir.

Ques. Was there not some dispute in respect to the item of hauling on this bill?

Ans. Yes, but I contended that my proposition was to deliver the lumber at Cumberland, on the car.

Ques. Was anybody else present in your counting-room when the conversation took place?

Ans. There was not.

Witness stated that where he used the words "only such as suited them," he intended to use the words "only that which was merchantable."

H. P. TASKER.

WM. R. McCULLEY sworn.

By Mr. Poe.

Ques. Where did you live and what was your employment in November, 1868?

Ans. I lived in Cumberland. I was book-keeper and cashier for H. P. Tasker & Co.

Ques. Look at those two papers (marked receipts of H. P. Tasker, $1,200 and $150.) are they in your hand-writing?

Ans. Neither of them is in my hand-writing.

Ques. Look at that paper (marked H. P. Tasker's receipt, $293.17,) is that in your hand-writing?

Ans. It is.

Ques. Do you make out the bills?

Ans. Yes, sir.

Ques. Are the two first bills in the hand-writing of Mr. Tasker or anybody connected with his establishment?

Ans. I think not. I do not know the hand-writing.

Ques. Are you aware of any sales of articles mentioned in those bills?

Ans. No, sir; I know nothing about the sales.

Ques. State from your books what transactions you had with the Chesapeake and Ohio Canal Company in November, 1868?

Ans. The bill of $293.17 embraces all the transactions I know of with that Company with the exception of a bill made in December 23d for tow lines and bow lines of $95, paid in January, 1869.

Ques. When was the $293.17 bill paid?

Ans. On the 9th of November. It is my impression that Mr. Sprigg paid it, but am not sure whether he or Col. Spates paid it. They were together when the last bill was paid.

Ques. Do your books show no such transaction as this, (referring to the two first bills for $1,200 and $150?)

Ans. No, sir.

Ques. Who attended to the lumber yard?

Ans. A man named Male.

Cross-Examination by Mr. Schley.

Ques. By whom was the $293.17 bill paid?
Ans. I do not recollect whether by Col. Spates or Mr. Sprigg.

Ques. Do you recollect whether they were both there when the bill was paid on the 9th of November?
Ans. I do not. I do not recollect who was in the room when it was paid. I have not been well for a long time and cannot trust my memory.

Ques. Do you recollect or not whether Mr. Tasker was in the counting-room when that bill was paid?
Ans. I do not.

Ques. Or whether there was any difficulty made about dividing the bill?
Ans. I recollect none. I have no recollection of anything that occurred at that time.

Ques. If there had been a difficulty, would not it likely have impressed itself on your mind?
Ans. If there had been any material difficulty in reference to the account, of course I would be likely to have remembered it.

Ques. Do you not recollect that there was a difficulty, and Mr. Tasker remarked, after handing to Mr. Spates two bill-heads, that he would be glad to get rid of the difficulty?
Ans. It might have occurred, but I do not remember it.

Ques. Did you hear Col. Spates ask Mr. Tasker for two bill-heads, so as to correct that account, and if so, did you see Mr. Tasker hand them to him?
Ans. No; my impression was Colonel Spates got the extra bill-heads at the time of the payment of $95 in January.

Ques. Who furnished the information from which you made the entries of lumber?
Ans. Male generally brought them from the yard, which was off from the office, down the railroad. I was guided by that alone.

Ques. When the dissolution took place, or prior to it, was there any trouble about a deficiency?
Ans. There was about a deficiency of 30,000 or 40,000 feet.

Ques. How did the firm know what lumber went into the yard?
Ans. There was a bill accompanying each cargo from the mill, and from those bills it was entered up at the office.

Ques. When where you at the office?
Ans. I went down at 7 o'clock, left for dinner at 12, and returned about one o'clock.

Ques. Did the orders emanate from the firm for all the lumber?
Ans. Yes, sir.

Ques. On what mill?
Ans. Generally on Tasker's mill.

Ques. Do you know who carries on the mill there for him?
Ans. His brother was superintendent, managing it.

By Mr. Poe.

Ques. You said, in answer to a question, that it was your impression that Col. Spates got the extra billheads at the payment of the last bill?
Ans. That is my impression, but am not certain.

Ques. But you mean to say that either at the one time or the other he got the extra heads?
Ans. My impression is it was the latter, but it might have been the former. I am clear that he did get them at one time or the other.

Ques. Was the apparent deficiency of lumber ever corrected?
Ans. I do not think there was ever a settlement of it. I think, by an understanding between Mr. Tasker and the present firm, there was a re-measurement, but no record was made of it, and I do not know the result.

W. R. McCULLEY.

MARCH 8TH, 1870.

The Committee met at 4.30 o'clock P. M.
Present as before.

JOHN PATTERSON sworn.

By Mr. Poe.

Ques. Where do you reside?
Ans. In Allegany county.

Ques. What is your occupation?
Ans. I am clerk in the office of the county clerk.

Ques. Are you an acquaintance of Col. Spates?
Ans. I know him.

Ques. Intimately?
Ans. I know him as well as any person in our county.

Ques. Have you ever been employed by him to do writing?
Ans. Yes, sir.

Ques. Are these papers in your handwriting? (Receipts of H. P. Tasker for $1,200 and $150.)
Ans. Yes, sir.

Ques. Please to state to the Committee for whom you prepared those papers?
Ans. I copied them for Mr. Spates.

Ques. After you copied them what did you do with them?
Ans. I delivered them to Mr. Spates.

Ques. Did you copy the signature as well as the body of the bills?
Ans. The whole is in my handwriting.

Ques. What were they copied from?
Ans. From just what is written on those bills.

Ques. Did Mr. Spates furnish you those billheads to copy them on?
Ans. I think he did.

Ques. After you copied them did you deliver them to him?
Ans. I left them in his possession.

Ques. Were those stamps on them at the time you delivered them to him?
Ans. The cancellation on one of the stamps looks like my handwriting, but I am not able to speak positively about the stamps.

Ques. What became of the originals from which you copied them?
Ans. I left them together with these papers.

Ques. Do you know in whose handwriting the originals were?
Ans. I do not. It was not Mr. Spates' handwriting.

Cross-Examination by Mr. Schley.

Ques. Are these the copies of the papers Mr. Spates put in your hands, and are the originals the same?
Ans. Yes, sir.

Ques. Were you in the habit of doing a good deal of writing for Mr. Spates at various times?
Ans. Yes, sir.

Ques. Have you ever done any in his office, when he was President of the Canal Company?
Ans. Frequently.

J. W. R. PATTERSON.

EZEKIEL A. MALE sworn.

By Mr. Gordon.

Ques. At what were you engaged in the months of October and November, 1868?
Ans. I was in the employ of Mr. Tasker, attending his lumber yard.

Ques. Do you know of any lumber furnished to the Canal Company, and if so, how much?

Ans. There was some furnished, I do not know exactly the amount.

Ques. What did you do with it?

Ans. I generally returned it to Mr. McCulley?

Ques. Did you return this particular lumber to him?

Ans. I returned all that was sold the Canal Company to him.

Cross-Examination by Mr. Schley.

Ques. What do you mean by saying you returned it to Mr. McCulley?

A. I returned all that came under my notice. There was one car load shipped from the depot which did not come under my notice.

Ques. That which came under your notice was confined to the lumber yard?

Ans. Yes, sir.

By Mr. Gordon.

Ques. What kind of lumber was that shipped from the depot?

Ans. It was long lumber which came down on double trucks.

By Mr. Schley.

Ques. Did you ever know of any other lumber going to the Canal Company?

Ans. No, sir.

Ques. Do you not recollect Col. Spates and Mr. Sprigg coming from Brengle's store towards Rhind's corner, when you were on the other side of the street, and Mr. Sprigg calling you over and asking you anything in regard to lumber for the Canal Company, on cars from Tasker's, and did you, or did you not, tell him you saw $3\frac{1}{2}$ car loads for the Canal Company, because you saw on the car "for the Canal Company?"

Ans. No, sir.

Ques. Was the question not put to you by Mr. Sprigg, "How do you know?" and you then remarked to him, that they marked for the Canal Company?

Ans. No, sir.

Ques. Did not Mr. Sprigg ask you how you came at the number of feet and did you not reply that you had to take the measurement of the mill?

Ans. I have no recollection of any such conversation. I never spoke to Mr. Sprigg, as I know of, in Cumberland until a week ago upon that subject.

Ques. Did you not say to George Hughes that you knew of three and one-half car loads of lumber that went to the Canal Company from Tasker's mill?

Ans. No. I told Hughes there was a car load of lumber on double trucks, a part of which was for the Canal Company and part for our yard, but did not tell him there were 3½ loads.

EZEKIEL A. MALE.

CHARGE No. 5.

WEDNESDAY, March 9th, 1870.

The Committee met at 4 P. M.

Present as before.

AMOS THOMAS sworn.

By Mr. Poe.

Ques. Were you Superintendent of the Monocacy Division of the Chesapeake and Ohio Canal Company in April and May, 1869?

Ans. Yes, sir.

Ques. Did you apply to your Company for a scow and mud machine for your Division in the Spring of 1869?

Ans. Yes, sir.

Ques. Please to state whether Mr. Spates, President of the Company, undertook to have the scow furnished from Cumberland, and whether you drew from the Canal Company the money to pay for it?

Ans. Mr. Spates undertook to furnish the scow. The money never passed through my hands. My father brought me the voucher for the $350 paid for the scow.

Ques. Did he get the voucher from Mr. Spates?

Ans. I do not know.

Ques. Did you return that voucher to the office of the Canal Company with your abstract?

Ans. I did.

Ques. Look at the paper now shown to you, (marked receipt of Henry Snyder for $350,) and see whether that is the voucher?

Ans. That looks like my No. 49. If that is the voucher I sent to the office it is the one he gave me.

Ques. Is this your monthly abstract (marked abstract of Amos Thomas for April, 1869?)

Ans. Yes, sir.

Ques. Are the words, Henry Snyder, $350, in your hand-writing, on the list of bills paid?

Ans. They are.

Ques. Did you charge the bill and receipt of Henry Snyder amongst your expenditures for that month?

Ans. Yes, sir.

Ques. Did you file the receipt as a voucher?

Ans. I did.

Cross-Examination by Mr. Schley.

Ques. Did you get the scow and mud machine?

Ans. Yes, sir.

Ques. How long did you have it before it was paid for?

Ans. I had it some time; I don't remember how long.

Ques. Look at that paper (marked letter of Amos Thomas, March 30, 1869,) and see if it is your letter?

Ans. It is.

Ques. Please read it?

Ans. "March 30th, 1869. To the President and Directors of Chesapeake and Ohio Canal: The Monocacy Division, under my charge, is in complete and good navigable condition. I let the water on the entire Division 12th inst. I am progressing slowly. I will, as soon as the water in the Potomac river will permit, I shall finish the riprapping at that point along the canal at Weverton, which I think ought to be done as soon as possible. Scow and mud machine is very badly wanting.

Most respectfully,

(Signed) AMOS THOMAS.
Sup't."

Ques. Look at that paper (marked letter of Amos Thomas, May 3d, 1869,) and see if it is your letter?

Ans. Yes, sir.

Ques. Please read it?

Ans. "May 3rd, 1869. To the President and Directors of Chesapeake and Ohio Canal Company: I respectfully report that the Monocacy Division, under my charge, has been in a good, navigable condition up to date. The heavy rains and high waters early in April caused a portion of the northern side of the culvert east of the Point of Rocks to give way, but by timely notice prevented any interruption of navigation. I have no scow on that part of the Division until to-day. I get an old one sent me by the President, and now, as soon as possible, I will get the kind of stone to repair the culvert, so no further trouble may be expected from it. I am also laboring under great disadvantage for the want of a mud machine to keep clear the mud from the mouth of the feeder at dam No. 3. * * *

(Signed,) AMOS THOMAS,
Sup't."

Ques. Was the scow worth $350?
Ans. It was. I thought it cheap at that. It was not a new scow.

AMOS THOMAS.

Mr. Schley offered in evidence the resolution of the Board of Directors, passed March 3rd, 1869, found on page 149, Proceedings of the President and Directors, as follows:

"On motion, it was ordered that the President and General Superintendent have constructed and built for the use of Monocacy, Antietam and other Divisions of the canal, one mud machine, also one scow, for the use of the Monocacy Division, said mud machine and scow to be paid for by the Superintendent of Monocacy Division upon the presentation of the bills of cost for the same by the President and General Superintendent."

HENRY SNYDER sworn.

By Mr. Poe.

Ques. Where do you live?
Ans. In Cumberland.
Ques. How long have you lived there?
Ans. Seventeen years.
Ques. What is your trade or business?
Ans. I work in the boat yard of Fred. Martin.
Ques. Did you work there in April, 1869?
Ans. I worked all the time for him.
Ques. Did you ever build a scow for the Chesapeake and Ohio Canal Company?
Ans. No, sir; never.
Ques. Did you ever sell a scow to that Company?
Ans. No.
Ques. Do you read and write English?
Ans. No, sir, not a word.
Ques. Do me the favor to write your name.
(Witness here wrote "Heinrich Schneider," on paper marked "H. S.")

Ques. Look at that paper, (marked receipt of Henry Snyder for $350.)
Ans. I never saw that paper until Mr. Gordon showed it to me.

Ques. Did you ever receive from the Canal Company $350 on that paper?
Ans. No, sir.

Ques. Is there any other Henry Snyder in Cumberland who is a boat builder?
Ans. My son is named Henry Snyder, but he is not able to build a boat. He is poor just as I am.

Ques. Did he ever build a scow for the Canal Company?
Ans. No.

Ques. Do you know any other Henry Snyder besides your son who is a boat builder?
Ans. No.

Ques. Do you know the boat builders pretty well in Cumberland?
Ans. I do.

Cross-Examination by Mr. Schley.

Ques. When was the first time you had your attention directed to this matter?
Ans. When Mr. Gordon came to the yard and showed me this bill.

Ques. How often did he come down?
Ans. One time.

Ques. Did he only show you one paper?
Ans. That is all.

Ques. Do you know how many boats the Canal Company has got?
Ans. I do not.

HEINOIH SCHNIDARE.

JAMES J. McHENRY sworn.

By Mr. Poe.

Ques. State where you live?
Ans. In Cumberland, Allegany county.

Ques. What is your profession?
Ans. I am a lawyer.

Ques. Look at that paper, (marked receipt of Henry Snyder, $350) and state to the Committee in whose handwriting it is?
Ans. It is in my handwriting with the exception of the signature.

Ques. State at whose instance you prepared that paper and the circumstances?

Ans. About a year and a half ago I was coming down Baltimore street, in Cumberland, in the afternoon, after the cars came in from Baltimore, and when I came to the corner of Baltimore and Centre streets, I saw Mr. Spates standing on the corner, and some one was with him. As I came up, Mr. Spates said, "Mack, I wish you would come in and make out a little bill for me. I want to pay this man, who wants to get his money to go home this evening." I don't pretend to give his language, but that is the impression what he said created on my mind. I went into the store of J. and T. Coulehan, and made out one bill, and Mr. Spates observed, "Make out another one. I have to keep duplicates." I did so, and afterwards he and I walked out the front door together, and the person who was with him went away with him.

Ques. Did he dictate the terms of the bill to you?
Ans. Yes, sir.

Ques. Did you know that Amos Thomas was Superintendent of the Monocacy Division at that time?
Ans. I did not. The whole of that information was derived from Mr. Spates.

Ques. Was the paper signed when it passed out of your hands?
Ans. It was not.

Ques. Was there any stamp on it?
Ans. There was not.

Ques. You are on terms of familiar intimacy with Mr. Spates, are you not?
Ans. I am. I have for the last eighteen years been in the habit of writing letters for Mr. Spates, and often making copies and fixing up papers time and again, so that asking this little favor was not an unusual thing.

Cross-Examination by Mr. Schley.

Ques. You have seen Henry Snyder here?
Ans. Yes, sir.

Ques. Was that the man with Mr. Spates?
Ans. It was not. The man with Mr. Spates was a stranger to me.

By Mr. Poe.

Ques. Do you know of any other Henry Snyder, a boat builder in Cumberland?
Ans. I do not.

Ques. How long have you lived in Cumberland?
Ans. Twenty-four years.

By Mr. Schley.

Ques. Do you recollect, or not, whether Mr. Spates told you where the man lived that was with him at that time?

Ans. There is an impression on my mind that he either said Hancock Division or Seneca Division.

By Mr. Poe.

Ques. You say you have lived in Cumberland twenty-four years; do you know Thomas Sheridan?

Ans. Very well.

Ques. Do you know any Thomas Sheridan engaged in boat building except Thomas Sheridan, the foreman of Mr. Weld?

Ans. I do not. He has a son of that name, a youth.

Ques. Might there be a man doing a job of work of that kind and you know nothing about it?

Ans. There might be, but there is no other Thomas Sheridan known to the community but Thomas Sheridan, the agent of Henry Thomas Weld.

By Mr. Schley.

Ques. Might there not have been a Thomas Sheridan building a boat in the yard of the Chesapeake and Ohio Canal Company and you not know it?

Ans. There might have been. There are a great many men there I do not know at all.

Ques. Did you ever know of two scows being built on the ground where the first wharf was, on the left hand side going from my office, when two men came there and built those scows, and afterwards disappeared?

Ans. I do recollect something of the kind, but do not know who they were.

By Mr. Poe.

Ques. Look at that bill of Thomas Sheridan's and see if you know the handwriting?

Ans. I cannot say whose handwriting it is.

By Mr. Gordon.

Ques. State whether the paper (marked True Copy of Record of Inquisition proved by Mr. McHenry) is in your handwriting?

Ans. It is all in my handwriting except the signature of the clerk.

Ques. Is that a correct copy?

Ans. It is. I made it out from the original papers.

J. J. McHENRY.

CHARGE No. 6.

BENJAMIN FAWCETT recalled.

By Mr. Poe.

Ques. Please turn to the journal, and show the resolution of the Board placing $10,000 in the hands of Mr. Spates for the condemnation of lands at Cumberland?

Ans. It is found in the proceedings of March 11th, 1868, on page 80, and is as follows: "Ordered, that the sum of $10,000 be advanced to the President, to be applied to the cost and expenses attending the condemnation of land at Cumberland, Md., required for the extension of the Canal and basin at that place."

Ques. When the expenditure of this $10,000 was accounted for were you the clerk of the Company?

Ans. I was.

Ques. Take this bundle of papers and state whether those constitute the vouchers for the expenditure of that $10,000 furnished to the President?

Ans. They are.

Ques. Did they exceed the amount of $10,000?

Ans. They did by $850.77.

Ques. Was that amount subsequently paid to Mr. Spates?

Ans. It was.

Ques. Is that the receipt of Mr. Spates for that money (marked Receipt of Alfred Spates for $850.77)?

Ans. It is.

Ques. When was it paid?

Ans. On the 4th or 5th of February, 1869?

Ques. Were these vouchers brought to the office of the Company by Mr. Spates?

Ans. They were presented by him to the Board January 7th, 1869, as shown by resolution on page 130, Journal of Proceedings.

Ques. Look at that paper, (marked altered copy of Record of Inquisition,) and state whether that was among the vouchers?

Ans. That was one of them.

(Mr. Poe called the attention of the Committee to the change of the word "six" to "eight," on page 1 of this copy, the change of the figure "6" to the figure "8" on page 3, the date "1866" left unaltered on the fourth page, the only place in the record. The insertion of the word "late" before "sheriff," on the 5th page, and the change of the word "six" to "eight," and the insertion of the word "late" before "sheriff," on page 7, the alteration of the figure "6" to "8" in four places on the 8th page.)

Mr. Poe also offered in evidence the original receipt of J. Philip Roman, attorney for the Canal Company, to the Rose Hill Wharf Company, for condemnation in the Weld case, dated Sept. 21st, 1866.

By Mr. Poe.

Ques. Were you clerk of the Company when that inquisition in the Weld case was filed in the office?

Ans. I was.

Ques. Did Mr. Spates receive the allowance on that inquisition of $739?

Ans. He did.

Ques. Did that paper remain in your official custody from that time until this?

Ans. It did, except when the Committee had it.

Ques. When it first came in possession of the Committee had those alterations been made, and was it in the condition it now is?

Ans. Precisely as it is now.

Ques. Was the paper now shown to you marked "list of vouchers," on top of the bundle of vouchers presented by Mr. Spates?

Ans. It was.

Ques. Was it in the condition it now is?

Ans. It was, except the red ink figures.

Mr. Poe offered in evidence paper marked, Certificate of Deposit of $739.

No cross-examination.

BENJ. FAWCETT.

CHARGE No. 7.

PATRICK MURRAY sworn.

By Mr. Poe.

Ques. Where do you live?

Ans. Mount Savage, Allegany county.

Ques. Had you a claim against the Chesapeake and Ohio Canal Company for scrip and acceptances?

Ans. Yes, sir.

Ques. How did it arise?

Ans. For work I did on the Canal between the years 1837 and 1842.

Ques. Tell the Committee how you came to recover that judgment and to get payment of a part of it, and from whom you got it?

Ans. When Mr. Spates was President I appealed to him, being thrown out of work, to get the money owing to me. He promised he would do so, but some time afterward, when I spoke to him again I thought he was a little cool. I then appealed to Mr. Roman, and left the papers with him. He promised me to get judgment, which he did.

Ques. What took place between you and Mr. Spates after the judgment?

Ans. Nothing more than that I got a check in Mr. Roman's room at the banking house for $324?

Ques. Was Mr. Spates there?

Ans. Yes, sir.

Ques. Did you execute a receipt for it?

Ans. Yes, sir.

Cross-Examination by Mr. Schley.

Ques. Who gave you the check for the money?

Ans. I think Mr. Roman wrote it and Mr. Spates signed it.

Ques. Was Mr. Spates there at the time?

Ans. He was.

Ques. Did you draw the money on the same day?

Ans. Yes, sir.

Ques. Was Mr. Spates there when it was paid?

Ans. Not when it was paid. I went to the bank to get the money.

Ques. Where did you get the check?

Ans. In Roman's office.

Ques. Look at the back of the check and see whether that is your hand-writing?

Ans. I think so.

(Mr. Schley offered in evidence the hand-writing of the check to prove that J. Philip Roman made the transaction himself as attorney of the Canal Company.)

By Mr. Clarke.

Ques. Did you consider this payment of $324 in final discharge of your claim for upwards of $1,200, or in part payment?

Ans. I considered it only in part payment of the first amount of $927.12.

By Mr. Poe.

Ques. Were you not something of a politician about that time, and did not you have considerable political influence at Mount Savage?

Ans. I held the office of magistrate and constable, but did not consider myself a politician, and do not know that I could influence many votes.

Ques. You said it was through sympathy you got this much; was it on account of any political influence you promised to exert?

Ans. I never promised to exert any political influence, but said if anything came in my power that I could do I would do it.

By Mr. Schley.

Ques. Who got the judgment for you?

Ans. I cannot say. He told me to leave my papers with him, and he would get me a judgment. He afterwards told me he had to pay a lawyer $5 to get the judgment, and I had to pay the lawyer $5 for that judgment.

PATRICK MURRY.

CHARGE No. 8.

HENRY McKEON sworn.

By Mr. Gordon.

Ques. Were you the clerk of the corporation of Cumberland in March, 1868?

Ans. I was.

Ques. Do you know anything about an account that was presented to the corporation for the removal of boats from the Canal basin?

Ans. That account was presented in May.

Ques. Have you got that paper, and if so, produce it?

Ans. I have, and produce it, (marked statement and order as to removal of boats.)

Ques. Who presented that paper to the Council?

Ans. I think Mr. Spates brought it in, but am not positive.

Ques. Do you know whose handwriting it is?

Ans I do not.

Ques. Did Mr. Spates get any money on that paper?

Ans. I issued a draft for the amount called for—$540—payable four months after date.

Cross-Examination by Mr. Schley.

Ques. Do you say that Mr. Spates handed that paper to you?

Ans. No sir, I do not say that.

Ques. Was Mr. Spates in the council chamber?
Ans. I think so.

Ques. Do you know how you got possession of that paper?
Ans. I know it came from the Committee on Finance or Committee on Accounts.

Ques. When was the first time of that the paper in the council chamber, who did you see first in possession of it?
Ans. I think it was some member of the council. I do not recollect who.

Ques. Do you recollect Asa Willison making some remarks on that subject?
Ans. I do.

Ques. Do you recollect, while speaking, he was referring to a paper before him on which he had some calculations roughly made, and handed it to you?
Ans. I do not.

Ques. Was or was not that paper left on Willison's desk?
Ans. I do not think so.

Ques. Is the order on the second page in your handwriting?
Ans. It is not. I think it is in Andrew Gonder's handwriting.

Ques. Was that order on it when it was given to you?
Ans. It was.

Ques. Do you know whether the Cumberland Coal and Iron Company paid their $160.
Ans. They did not.

HENRY McKEON.

CHARGE No. 8.

THURSDAY, March 10, 1870.

The Committee met at 9½ o'clock, A. M.

Present as before.

BENJAMIN FAWCETT recalled.

By Mr. Poe.

Ques. State whether or not the paper (marked abstract of R. M. Sprigg for April, 1868,) and paper (marked receipt of A. L. Miller for $1,452) were returned to the office by the Superintendent of the Cumberland Division.
Ans. They were.

(Mr. Poe stated that he had no proof of the payment of $160 by the Cumberland Coal and Iron Company.)

Ques. Was there any entry in the records of the office to show that Mr. Spates had accounted for the sum of $540, received from the corporation of Cumberland, or any part of it?

Ans. I have never received it or known any part of it being paid.

Cross-Examination by Mr. Schley.

Ques. Have you any evidence that the Canal Company is entitled to that $540?

Ans. No, sir. I know nothing about the transaction except from the papers. It took place before I came into office?

Ques. When did you go into office?

Ans. On the 1st day of May, 1868.

Ques. You say you found this paper when you came in (marked abstract of R. M. Sprigg for April, 1868,) what is the date on the back of it?

Ans. It was received on the 14th of May, after I came there, but the transaction took place before I went into office.

Mr. Schley offered in evidence the endorsement of this paper, "Examined and adproved Sept. 2nd. Jno. B. Thomas and Esau Pickerell, Comm's on Accounts."

BENJ. FAWCETT.

CHARGE No. 5.

MARCH 10, 1870.

JOHN B. THOMAS sworn.

By Mr. Poe.

Ques. Were you a director in the Canal Company in the spring of 1869?

Ans. I was.

Ques. Do you recollect the furnishing of a scow for the Monocacy Division of which your son is Superintendent?

Ans. I do. It was furnished some time in the spring of that year

Ques. Please state what you recollect about it?

Ans. I paid Mr. Spates $350 for that scow, received a voucher from him for that amount and returned it to my son.

Ques. Is that the voucher?

Ans. I could not say whether it is or not, but $350 is the amount.

Ques. From whom did you receive the money?

Ans. It was appropriated by the Board, and money was appropriated at the same time to pay for a mud machine?

Ques. Did you take up the money to pay for the mud machine?
Ans. I did. It amounted to about $1,500.

Ques. What did you do with that money?

Ans. I gave it to the Superintendent and he took it to town and deposited it in the Central National Bank at Frederick.

Ques. Do you know anything of the distribution of that money by your son?

Ans. I know that he received the vouchers for the mud machine because he showed it to me.

Cross-Examination by Mr. Schley.

Ques. You were a director you say in the Canal Company. Were you on the Committee on Accounts?

Ans. I was.

Ques. Look at the back of that abstract, and state whether the signature is yours?

Ans. It is. I examined all the abstracts with care, as they came in, and approved them after examination.

Ques. After the Committee on Accounts had endorsed them were they submitted to the Board and passed by them?

Ans. They were always submitted to the Board afterwards.

By Mr. Gordon.

Ques. How did you make the examinations of the accounts; did you go behind the vouchers or take them as correct?

Ans. We merely examined the abstracts by the vouchers, supposing the vouchers to be correct. Mr. Pickerell would read off the vouchers. I would check them off on the abstract, and then add up the amounts.

By Mr. Poe.

Ques. But whether a voucher was a genuine one or not, you had no means of determining?

Ans. We had not.

By Mr. Gordon.

Ques. Do you recollect examining the claim of the President for the distribution of $10,000?

Ans. I do.

Ques. Was it afterwards submitted to the Board?

Ans. It was, and approved by them.

By Mr. Schley.

Ques. Was not the mud machine delivered, as well as the scow, before it was paid for?

Ans. Yes, sir; both of them—at least my son told me the mud machine was on his Division before I paid Mr. Spates for the voucher.

By Mr. Gordon.

Ques. Do you know where the scow and mud machine were gotten?

Ans. I do not; but am under the impression that they came from Cumberland, because they ordered to be made there. Mr. Sprigg had them sent down, and my son met the men who had charge of them, I think, at the big tunnel, and brought them down.

By Mr. Schley.

Ques. Do you not recollect that Mr. Spates told you he could not build one, but he had bought a second-hand scow?

Ans. It does appear that he did say so.

JOHN B. THOMAS.

CHARGE No. 5.

March 10th, 1870.

JOHN SNYDER sworn.

By Mr. Poe.

Ques. Where do you live?
Ans. In Cumberland.

Ques. What is your business?
Ans. Boat and scow building.

Ques. Have you a partner?
Ans. I have none know. I had a partner about a year ago named Bearice.

Ques. What was the name of the firm?
Ans. John Snyder & Co.

Ques. When did the partnership cease?
Ans. In July, 1869.

Ques. Where you in partnership in May, 1869?
Ans. I was.

Ques. You were before the Committee composed of Messrs. Gordon, Thompson, Biser and myself, in Cumberland, were you not?
Ans. I was.

Ques. Do you recollect the statements you made at that time?
Ans. Very well; and I am verry sorry to tell you the statement I made then was false, and I am prepared to correct it.

Ques. You stated at that time that your firm was employed by Col. Spates to do the corking, and you furnished the oakum and pitch, for all of which you received $25, but that the other items of the bill you did not furnish, and were not paid for. Look at that bill and correct your former statement?

Ans. They were making a new basin, and there was an engine to be put up, and I had orders to do the work. I put up the engine, and did some other work at the same time, and did work for the engineer whenever called on by him. At the end of the month, when I came to make out my bill, I did not know how to charge for the work, except the $25, and Col. Spates told me to make it out for the mud machine, and I did so.

Ques. In what month was that?

Ans. I cannot recollect. It was early in the spring. It might have been in March, and was not as late as May.

Ques. Did you paint the mud machine?
Ans. I did not.

Ques. Did you get paid for painting the mud machine?
Ans. I do not think I did.

Ques. Did you work on the mud machine as carpenter?

Ans. I did the work for the amount the receipt calls for, and it was charged to the mud machine. I did it in other ways, and charged it, by direction of the President, to the mud machine.

Ques. Did you furnish the oakum, pitch and caulking?
Ans. I did.

By Mr. Gordon.

Ques. Have you had any conversation with Col. Spates lately?

Ans. I have seen him twice since I came down, but did not talk with him about this matter then or before I came down.

Ques. Did you talk with Mr. Sprigg about it?
Ans. I did not.

By Mr. Poe.

Ques. Did you do twenty-nine days work as carpenter?
Ans. I did not do it myself but had it done by my hands.

Ques. Do you know who made out that bill?
Ans. It was made out by one of the supervisors.

Ques. Is it Mr. Spriggs' handwriting?

Ans. I would not be positive, but I know the signature is in my handwriting.

(Mr. Spates admitted that the bill was made out by John W. Patterson.)

Cross-Examination by Mr. Schley.

Ques. At the time you were before the Committee in Cumberland did or did they not give you a gold pen, and ask you to write your name?

Ans. They did.

Ques. After you wrote your name, did they not take up this paper and show you the signature, and tell you that was not your signature?

Ans. They did.

Ques. Did you tell them it was your signature?

Ans. I did, and told them I wrote it with a pen I used all the year round. They got me to write my hand twice, and insisted after comparing it that it was not my signature. I was on a little spree while I was doing the work, and there is where the whole secret lies.

By Mr. Schley.

Ques. Did Col. Spates pay you that money?

Ans. He did, and I gave him that receipt.

Messrs. Gordon and Poe admitted that evidence of the witness was not sufficient to sustain the charge so far as he was concerned.

JOHN SNYDER.

CHARGE No. 6.

MARCH 10th, 1870.

PERCY ROLAND sworn.

By Mr. Gordon.

Ques. What is your employment?

Ans. I am deputy clerk of the Circuit Court for Allegany county.

Ques. State whether you made out the copy of the record, (marked altered copy of record of inquisition) and whether it was made out as it is now, or whether there have been any changes made in it since you made it out?

Ans. The record is in my handwriting. There are some changes in it. The work "six," on page one, has been changed to "eight," and there are also changes on the third, fifth, sixth, seventh and eighth pages.

Ques. See if you find the word "late" interpolated in a different handwriting three times before the word sheriff?

Ans. I do.

Ques. Was that a correct transcript from the record in the office when it passed out of your hands?

Ans. It was when I handed it to Mr. Resley, the clerk.

Ques. Do you know who took it out of the office?

Ans. I do not of my own knowledge.

Ques. Are the alterations made in the handwriting of any of the clerks in the office?

Ans. They are not.

Ques. Do you know who ordered the transcript to be made out?

Ans. No, sir.

By Mr. Clarke.

Ques. You say the word "eight" is changed from "six." How do you know the word "six" was there?

Ans. On the first page it is not entirely erased, and I recollect it from making a copy of it.

By Mr. Schley.

Ques. Do you recollect the date of all the papers you copy?
Ans. I do not.

By Mr. Poe.

Ques. Were you present in the vault of the office when the transscript was compared with the original by Mr. Resley and myself?

Ans. I was. Mr. Gordon was there also.

Ques. On page four is not the sixty-six in your handwriting?
Ans. I think it is.

Cross-Examination by Mr. Schley.

Ques. Look at the endorsement "Filed March 9th, 1868," is that in your handwriting?

Ans. It is in my handwriting, except the eight, which has been changed from six.

Ques. When did you make out this copy?
Ans. I do not recollect the date.

Ques. How long have you been in the clerk's office?
Ans. Since March, 1868.

Ques. What does the endorsement mean?
Ans. The date when the original inquisition was filed in the office.

PERCIVAL ROWLAND.

CHARGE No. 6.

JOHN PATTERSON re-called.

By Mr. Poe.

Ques. Look at the paper (marked List of Vouchers,) and state in whose handwriting it is?

Ans. I think it is mine.

Ques. For whom did you make it out?

Ans. I do not know I do not remember ever seeing it before. If it is not in my hand-writing it is a very good copy of it.

Ques. Do you recollect making it out for Mr. Spates?

Ans. I do not.

By Mr. Gordon.

Ques. You frequently did copying for him, did you not?

Ans. Yes, sir.

By Mr. Schley.

Ques. You say you are in the habit of writing for Mr. Spates?

Ans I am; but have no recollection of that paper.

Ques. Is that paper in your hand-writing? (bill of John Snyder & Co.)

Ans. Yes, sir.

J. W. R. PATTERSON.

CHARGE No. 9.

MARCH 10, 1870.

DR. J. J. BRUCE recalled.

By Mr. Poe.

Ques. Please look at that account, (marked J. J. Bruce, for lumber, No. 1,) and state whether or not you furnished the lumber charged in that bill to Col. Alfred Spates?

Ans. Yes, sir; we furnished it for Mr. Spates' use.

Ques. Do you know what was done with that lumber?

Ans. It was used in making improvements upon Mr. Spates' property.

Ques. How do you know that?

Ans. The lumber was hauled by my teams and delivered to Mr. Spates, and I saw the workmen putting it up.

Ques. By whom were you paid?

Ans. By Mr. Sprigg. It was afterwards included by direction of Mr. Spates in the Canal Company's account, and he stated he would arrange it with the Board.

Ques. When were the two items $576.20 and $68.74 made?

Ans. At different times. The first in June and July, the last in September.

Ques. Look at the paper (marked Receipt of R. M. Sprigg from J. J. Bruce for $873.61, No. 1,) and state whether it includes the $576.20 sold to Col. Spates and delivered to him?

Ans. It does.

Ques. Look at the paper (marked Receipt of R. M. Sprigg from J. J. Bruce, No. 2,) and state whether that includes the $68.74 sold to Col. Spates, and delivered to him?

Ans. It does. The assumpsit of the two amounts is shown on " Bill of J. J. Bruce for lumber, No. 2."

Mr. Poe offered in evidence abstract of R. M. Sprigg, for July, 1868, and called attention to the first item on page 3, " Bruce J. J. $873.61, of which witness testified $576.20 was for lumber bought and used by Mr. Spates.

Cross-Examination by Mr. Schley.

Ques. Did Mr. Spates order the lumber charged on that bill (Receipt No. 1)?

Ans. My impression is that Mr. Berston, the foreman, ordered it in Mr. Spates' name.

Ques. Was that bill made out afterwards, (bill No. 1)?

Ans. It was. I made it out at the instance of Mr. Gordon.

By Mr. Poe.

Ques. Did the account stand originally against Mr. Spates?

Ans. It did.

Ques. Are those accounts a transcript of the accounts on your books?

Ans. They are.

J. J. BRUCE.

BENJAMIN FAWCETT recalled.

By Mr. Poe.

Ques. Do you know whether or not Mr. Spates, late President of the Company, has accounted for the sum of $644.90 which appears to have been paid by Mr. Sprigg, Superintendent of the Cumberland Division, in July and September, 1868, for lumber furnished by Mr. Bruce to Mr. Spates for his own account, and charged to and paid by the Chesapeake and Ohio Canal Company?

Ans. I have no knowledge of it. There is nothing that I have ever seen on the books to show that he has accounted for it.

Ques. If any money had been paid in on that account, would it have come through your hands?

Ans. It would.

Cross-Examination by Mr. Schley.

Ques. Do you examine into the details of all lumber returned on the various abstracts to ascertain what was done with it?

Ans. I do not.

Ques. Do you not know that for the $644.90, an equal amount of lumber representing that sum had been used in Cumberland?

Ans. I do not.

Ques. If Mr. Sprigg had purchased lumber to that amount, would it properly have come in his monthly abstract?

Ans. It would.

Ques. Do you recollect or not whether there was any amounts returned for iron in that Cumberland Division?

Ans. I do not.

Ques. Is it usual for a Superintendent to make an exchange of lumber in his possession for a particular kind he could not get except from a third party?

Ans. That would be an irregular proceeding.

Ques. Do you know whether there has been any exchange of lumber with outside persons on the Cumberland Division since the present Board came in?

Ans. Not to my knowledge.

Ques. Were you clerk of the Company when the office was removed from Washington to Annapolis?

Ans. I was.

Ques. What became of the furniture?

Ans. Part of it was sold and part is still at the auctioneer's establishment, for which I have never received any return; part was taken to the Collector's office at Georgetown, and part to furnish a dwelling house on the Georgetown Division, where the hands boarded. There has been no annual report made since the furniture was disposed of. It will be accounted for on the next report.

Ques. Did the wagon of Mr. Thompson, one of the Directors, come there and take away some of the furniture?

Ans. It did. He was to give me what it was worth. There was a carpet and bureau taken away by the wagon.

Ques. Did you make a memorandum of what was taken away?

Ans. I did not. It was taken away in my absence.

Ques. By whose authority was the furniture removed?

Ans. By understanding of the Board. I had a conversation about it with Messrs. Thompson, Gormon and Condy, who were the Committee appointed by the Board for the removal of the office and the disposition of the furniture.

Ques. State what particular furniture was in the President's room?

Ans. A carpet, bureau with a glass on it, wash stand and bowl, sofa, secretary or book case, and a half-dozen chairs.

By Mr. Gordon.

Ques. When was the office finally removed?

Ans. About the 20th of December.

Ques. Has that matter been called to the notice of the Board?

Ans. It has not.

BENJ. FAWCETT.

FRIDAY, March 11th, 1870.

The Committee met at 9 A. M., pursuant to adjournment.

Present as before.

Mr. Gordon offered in evidence papers marked as follows:

"Letter of Mr. Poe to Col. Spates, Nov'r 8th, 1869."

"Letter of Mr. Poe to Col. Spates, Nov'r 15th, 1869."

"Letter of Col. Spates to Mr. Poe, Nov'r 15th, 1869."

"Letter of Col. Spates to President and Directors of Chesapeake and Ohio Canal Company, Nov'r 16th, 1869."

"Letter of Mr. Gordon to Col. Spates, Sept. 14th, 1868, endorsement no part of testimony."

And stated that the testimony in chief would here be closed.

OFFICE CHESAPEAKE AND OHIO CANAL CO.,
WASHINGTON CITY, Nov. 8, 1869.

ALFRED SPATES, Esq.,

Dear Sir:—By a resolution of the Board of Directors of the Chesapeake and Ohio Canal Company, the accounts of the late President have been referred to the Committee of Accounts, and I have been directed to notify you that the Committee will assemble at the Revere House, in Cumberland, on Saturday morning next, the 13th inst., at 9 o'clock, to enter upon the discharge of their duty. If you can find it convenient to meet them at the time and place designated you will oblige them and

Your ob't serv't,

NEILSON POE, *Ch'n.*

CUMBERLAND, Nov. 15, 1869.
ALFRED SPATES, Esq.,
  Late President of the Chesapeake and Ohio Canal Co. :

 Dear Sir :—In compliance with your request the Committee on Accounts desire your explanation at present in reference to the following transactions:

 1. Your expenditure of the sum of $10,850.77, placed in your hands by resolutions of the Board of the 11th of March, 1868, and of the 4th of February, 1869—and especially the credits claimed by and allowed to you upon vouchers No. 8, being a payment of $324 to Patrick Murray upon a judgment; voucher No. 9, being an alleged payment to Henry Thomas Weld and wife of $739.62 on the 21st of Sept., 1868, in satisfaction of the damages appearing to have been found against the Company by a jury under an inquisition affirmed on the 24th of May, 1868, and voucher No. 10, being a bill of Daniel Duncan, late Sheriff, for fees in the same case. The allowance of $739.62 appears to have been made to you upon a certified copy of the record, which was altered so as to make appear that the proceeding was in 1868, when in fact it was in 1866. As this altered record was filed in the office of the Company by you, and passed by the then Committee of Accounts, at your instance, the Committee feel that a full explanation is equally due to yourself and the Company, although you have on the demand of the present President refunded the money.

 2. Your expenditure of the sums received by you from John Shay and Isaac R. Mans, Superintendents, in November, 1869.

 3. Your expenditure of the sum of $540 received by you from the corporation of Cumberland, in aid of the cleaning out of the basin at place.

 4. An explanation of the payment by the Chesapeake and Ohio Canal Company to J. J. Bruce of the sum of $576.20 on the 8th of August, 1868, and the further sum of $68.74 to the same firm on the 9th of October, 1868—the said two sums being for lumber bought for your account and used by you.

 As the Committee are absent from their homes, at great personal inconvenience, they will be obliged if you will give them an answer with as little delay as possible.

  By order of the Committee,
         N. POE, *Ch'n.*

CUMBERLAND, MD., November 15, 1869.
NEILSON POE, ESQ.,
  Chairman :

 My dear sir :—I received your note of 8th inst., passed to me by the bugler on the judge's stand at the Agricultural Fair grounds on the 11th inst., informing me that by a resolution of the Canal Board the accounts of the late President were referred to a Committee; that said Committee would proceed on Saturday, 13th inst., to enter on the discharge of their duty. Certainly a very general sort of notice.

I am informed that a majority of the Committee now here have expressed opinions decidedly hostile to me; have made threats of suits and prosecutions, and I well know that the entire influence of the Chesapeake and Ohio Canal Company was used against my nomination and election as State Senator. All, or nearly all the employees of the Canal who supported me as the Democratic nominee have been removed from the canal, and I have just learned that Daniel Wineow, lock keeper at Cumberland, has been removed this day by your Committee because he voted for me, and a man appointed in his stead who voted and used his influence against my election. After these repeated acts of vindictive persecutions, not only against myself, but also against my friends, on the part of a majority of your Committee, I do not feel it consistent with my self-respect to appear before your Committee.

Prior to my nomination, and before the election, very much the same charges as set forth in your note of 15th inst. were industriously circulated in circular and handbill form by the permission and the individual act of Mr. Gordon, your President, and now one of your Committee.

I have the documentary evidence to satisfy any unprejudiced Committee that all the charges set forth in your note of 15th instant are groundless, and have been instigated with no expectation of proving a misapplication of any funds in my hands as late President of the Chesapeake and Ohio Canal Company, but to gratify the private malice of my enemies.

After consultation with my friends, and believing a majority of the Committee have prejudged the matters set forth in your note of 15th inst., I shall decline to appear before your Committee, as I never made any such request of the Committee as set forth in your note of 15th inst.

Very respectfully, &c.,
ALFRED SPATES.

CUMBERLAND, MD., November 16th, 1869.

To the President and Directors,

Chesapeake and Ohio Canal Co.:

Gentlemen :—I have learned that your Board meets in this city to-day, and as I was advised yesterday that a Committee of your Board were here on Saturday and yesterday, taking statements of persons in regard to my official action whilst President of the Chesapeake and Ohio Canal Company, and as I was not invited to be present to cross-examine these persons, the names of whom I am ignorant, I respectfully request that after your special committee report to your Board, that you furnish to me a copy of the statement made by each person, with the names of said persons, that I may have a fair opportunity to answer the same.

Very respectfully, &c.,
ALFRED SPATES.

CUMBERLAND, Sept. 14th, 1869.

MR. ALFRED SPATES,

Sir :—It appears by the books and proceedings of the Chesapeake and Ohio Canal Company that the sum of ten thousand dollars was placed by that Company in your hands while you were its President for the purpose of paying for condemnation of land at Cumberland, and it also appears that in settling with the Canal Company for that sum of ten thousand dollars, you claimed and received credit for the sum of seven hundred and thirty-nine dollars paid by J. Philip Roman for the Canal Company, to Josiah H. Gordon, as attorney for Henry Thomas Weld and wife, for condemnation, in No. 163, Trials to April term, 1868, in the Circuit Court for Allegany County, being for $725, damages and the cost in the case of Weld and wife for the right of way for the towing bridge of the Rose Hill Wharf Company across the mouth of Wills' Creek.

It also appears by a receipt of J. Philip Roman, as attorney of the Canal Company to the Rose Hill Wharf Company, that Mr. Roman received said sum of money from the Wharf Company, and that it has therefore been paid by the Canal Company and the Wharf Company both, or else you have claimed and received a credit for that amount of money from the Canal Company which you did not pay and have no right to.

I would be glad to have your explanation of this matter at once, as I am required to make a report to the Committee of Accounts of the Canal Company, which is now waiting my reply.

Yours, &c.,

J. H. GORDON,
President of the Ches. and Ohio Canal Co.

No. 1.

FRIDAY, March 11th, 1870.

[The Committee met at 4 P. M., pursuant to adjournment.]

Present as before.

TESTIMONY FOR THE DEFENCE.

RICHARD M. SPRIGG sworn.

By Mr. Schley.

Ques. Where do you live?

Ans. In Cumberland.

Ques. How long have you lived there?

Ans. Three years from the 1st of April. I have lived in Allegany county nearly all my life.

Ques. How long have you been in the employment of the Chesapeake and Ohio Canal Company?

Ans. I went into office on the 1st day of December, 1866.

Ques. When Mr. Spates came into the office of President of the Company, were you in the employment of the Canal Company?

Ans. Yes, sir.

Ques. Are you in the employment of the Canal Company now?

Ans. No, sir.

Ques. When were you turned out?

Ans. On the 9th of September, 1869. I got my notice of discharge on the 20th of September.

Ques. What was your position?

Ans. Superintendent of the Cumberland Division.

Ques. Before you were displaced, was, or was not, a proposition made to you in which was stated the terms upon which you could remain in the office you occupied?

Ans. There was.

Ques. Who made that proposition to you?

Ans. William McCaig.

Ques. What was it?

Ans. He told me that if I would vote against Col. Spates as candidate for the Senate I could keep my place, that he had been sent to me by Mr. Gordon and his brother Thomas.

(Mr. Gordon objected to the introduction of this testimony, unless William McCaig be produced as a witness.)

Ques. How many ice breakers were built on the Cumberland Division in 1867?

Ans. Three.

Ques. Who built them?

Ans. I built two for the Canal Company, and I had a man to build the other named Sheridan.

Ques. Tell the Committee where those ice breakers were built?

Ans. Two at the carpenter shop in the Company's yard, and one in Mr. Weld's yard.

Ques. Where was the one built that this man Sheridan built?

Ans. At the carpenter shop on our side of the Canal.

Ques. Who got those ice breakers?

Ans. George Spates got one, Mans got one, and the other is on the Cumberland Division.

Ques. Did you, or not, get Weld's hands to aid you in completing the ice breaker built in his yard, and if so, why?

Ans. We were very much hurried with work, and I sent over and asked Sheridan if he would lend me some of his hands, and he told me he would if I paid them the same as our hands got.

Ques. Did you or not keep the time of the hands of Weld working on that ice breaker?

Ans. I never kept the time of any man on the Canal.

Ques. Whose business was it to keep the time?

Ans. The bosses always kept the time.

Ques. Did you, or not, settle with the agent of Weld for the amount due him for the hands?

Ans. I did.

Ques. How much money did you pay him?

Ans. I do not recollect how much now, but I paid him for all the time his hands worked there.

Ques. Look at that abstract (marked R. M. Sprigg, No. 11,) and see if it is yours?

Ans. It is. Here are the names of the hands of Mr. Weld: Hiram Sellers, Caspar Brenger, George Wigley, Thomas Read, William Mullen, James Callahan, Henry Drier and C. Shermesser.

Ques. State to the Committee to whom and how you paid the money due the hands of Mr. Weld.

Ans. I went to Sheridan's office with blank vouchers, and told him I had come down to settle with him. Cahill got the book. He has a banister and table on the inside. The banister divides his office from Sheridan's. I sat down. Cahill gave me the time, and I filled up these vouchers on his table; and, as I would fill them up, would hand them to Sheridan, who witnessed them, and after we got through and counted all up, I paid Sheridan the money.

Ques. Did you, or not, get any receipts for that money, except those receipts?

Ans. No, sir; that is the only evidence.

Ques. Did Mr. Cahill give you no receipts?

Ans. No, sir. I never asked for any.

Ques. You say you built two boats in the fall of 1867—one on the Weld side, and one in the Company's yard: who built the other?

Ans. A man named Thomas Sheridan that I hired to build it.

Ques. Who is the blacksmith that ironed these boats?

Ans. William Dowden.

Ques. Who gave you the plan for those ice breakers?

Ans. Col. Spates.

Ques. Was or was not Col. Spates there nearly all the time hurrying the hands?

Ans. He was.

Ques. Look at your abstract for November, 1867, and tell the Committee how many ice breakers you paid for in 1867?

Ans. Two.

Ques. Did or did not Col. Spates exercise, and require you to exercise great caution, whilst those ice breakers were building, that none of the expenses of this ice breaker which was being built by Thomas Sheridan should get into your account?

Ans. He did.

Ques. Did you, or not, pay for that ice breaker built by Thomas Sheridan?

Ans. I did not.

Ques. Did you know Thomas Sheridan well?

Ans. I knew him for a year before he built this boat, and have seen him several times since. I have not seen him for nearly a year.

Ques. Do you know where he now is?

Ans. He is out West. I have written a dozen letters at least, to find where he is but could not find him.

Cross-Examination by Mr. Gordon.

Ques. Did you say you had seen Thomas Sheridan since?

Ans. I saw him between six months and a year ago; he was then in that neighborhood.

By Mr. Poe.

Ques. How long does it take to build an ice breaker?

Ans. That depends upon the hands you put upon it.

Ques. In this case how long did it take?

Ans. From 15 to 20 days.

Ques. Did you furnish to Sheridan any of the capital or money with which he built this ice breaker?

Ans. No, sir.

Ques. Did you furnish him any of the lumber?

Ans. He bought the lumber himself.

Ques. Did you furnish any of the iron?

Ans. I furnished some of the iron and caulking for the boat.

Ques. Did you furnish any other materials?

Ans. I do not think I did.

Ques. Do you know from whom he bought his lumber?

Ans. I do not. I never inquired.

Ques. Was it not in the yard in which you were constantly employed?
Ans. I was there frequently.

Ques. Do you know from what lumber yard his lumber was hauled?
Ans. I do not.

Ques. Did you ever see any teams coming into the yard with lumber for him?
A. I did see some teams coming from the mountains. They were mountain teams.

Ques. Did he buy any lumber from Cumberland?
Ans. I do not know that he did. I never inquired.

Ques. How many hands had he?
Ans. Some five or six.

Ques. Do you know the names of any of the hands he employed?
Ans. I do not recollect. They were not the hands that we employed.

Ques. Do you know the names of any of the carpenters he employed?
Ans. I think there were two of the Company's hands that worked some for him, named Smeltzer, and Jimmy Nooman.

Ques. Was their time paid for by him, or by you as Superintendent?
Ans. By me.

Ques. Did he refund the money?
Ans. He did not.

Ques. How old a man was Thomas Sheridan?
Ans. I cannot tell.

Ques. Was he an American or foreigner?
Ans. I do not know.

Ques. Was he a married or single man?
Ans. I do not know.

Ques. Did he keep house in Cumberland?
Ans. I think not.

Ques. Did he board in Cumberland?
Ans. I suppose he did if he did not keep house. I do not know where he boarded.

Ques. You state that you knew him very well for a year before, and knew him for six months or a year afterwards, did you never ask him where he boarded?
Ans. No, sir.

Ques. You have written a dozen letters to find him since he left. State to whom you wrote?

Ans. I wrote to him and to other people. I could tell you if I was at home. I wrote to him at Wheeling, and Grafton, and Parkersburg, and a dozen different places but could not hear anything of him.

Ques. Was this ice breaker painted?
Ans. Yes, sir.

Ques. Can you name any painter who was employed on it?
Ans. I cannot. I was not there more than once or twice a week.

Ques. Before he engaged upon this ice breaker did you know where he lived?
Ans. I did not.

Ques. How did you come across him?
Ans. He came to me and asked me to give him work.

Ques. Do you know anybody in Cumberland who was acquainted with him?
Ans. I do not.

Ques. Did you ever see him in company with anybody in Cumberland?
Ans. I have seen him walking about the street, but did not pay attention as to who was with him.

Ques. Do you know what he was employed about before he came to you?
Ans. I do not.

Ques. Do you know where he came from to Cumberland?
Ans. I do not.

Ques. What reason have you to suppose he went to Parkersburg?
Ans. I heard it talked about in town. I heard some one say he had gone out on the railroad.

Ques. From whom did you hear that?
Ans. I do not recollect. I never charged my memory with it.

Ques. He must necessarily have had considerable transactions in Cumberland while building the boat?
Ans. I do not know anybody with whom he has had transactions.

Ques. What kind of lumber was used in building this boat?
Ans. Pine lumber, and some oak. A very little oak.

Ques. Did he employ a boss carpenter?
Ans. I do not suppose he did.

By Mr. Gordon.

Ques. How many days did Sellers work on that boat?
Ans. I do not recollect how many.

Ques. Do those receipts state the time correctly?
Ans. That is the time I paid Sheridan.

By Mr. Poe.

Ques. Did you ever see Sheridan's handwriting—the one who built this boat?
Ans. I do not think I ever did.

Ques. Do you know how he spells his name?
Ans. I never saw it, but it strikes me that he did not spell it like the other Sheridan.

Ques. Why does it strike you so?
Ans. Because he did not call it in the same way.

Ques. I wish you would try and recollect what carpenters were employed by this man.
Ans. I do not recollect. I had a good many hands to attend to and did not pay much attention to him.

By Mr. Gordon.

Ques. What part of the wharf did he build it on?
Ans. He built it between the lock and the carpenter shop, the only part that belonged to the Canal Company at that time.

Ques. Did Sheridan ever do any other work for the Canal Company?
Ans. No, sir. The next day after it was launched we started down the Canal to break the ice. The Sheridan ice breaker we started right off for Mans.

Ques. Were you at work on the other ice breaker at the same time he was at work on his?
Ans. Yes, sir.

Ques. How many hands did you work on the one you were building?
Ans. We had Sheridan's hands and a part of our hands. A part of our hands were at that time at work building lock gates.

Ques. Where were you building lock gates?
Ans. In the old carpenter shop.

Ques. Where did you build the other boat?
Ans. We built one at a time and sent it off. We worked at ours on the Weld side at the same time this man was building his on our side.

Ques. Where had you first met this man?

Ans. I do not remember.

Ques. Did you ever see him at work at any place before he worked for you?

Ans. No.

Ques. Did not your business require you to go round a good deal?

Ans. It did, but not to inquire where other people were working.

Ques. Did not it frequently bring you in contact with other people at work?

Ans. I did not have to go twice a year to other boat yards in the three years I was Superintendent.

By Mr. Poe.

Ques. You say you furnished to him some of the iron from the Canal Company's stores of iron, and did not charge it to Sheridan?

Ans. That was the understanding when he built the boat, that I was to furnish some iron and caulk it, and give him what lumber I could spare.

Ques. Was there nothing in your accounts to show what became of the iron that was applied to this ice breaker?

Ans. Nothing; but I charged the Company with what the boat cost over $800.

Ques. Take your abstract for November, 1867, and show where you charged the Division with the difference?

Ans. I suppose it all comes under the head "Tools and Boats."

Ques. You say $1,600 is all you charged for the two ice breakers. Where is anything to show any account of anything over $800?

Ans. What I got for him and what I got for myself is charged in the same bill.

Ques. How much of the iron did you furnish?

Ans. I did not furnish one-fourth of the iron.

Ques. Did he not get a good deal of the iron from Col. Spates?

Ans. I do not know where he got the balance.

Ques. How many ice breakers were there at that time on the Cumberland Division?

Ans. Two old ones, that were of no account in the world, which I repaired, but one broke in two breaking ice, and we put one out over the dam. I built two new ones, and sent them down the canal, and the last one I built for the Cumberland Division. By "putting it out over the dam," I mean thrown out as useless.

Re-Examination by Mr. Schley.

Ques. Are there not a great many people in Cumberland you do not know?

Ans. There are.

Ques. Is not the population a floating one, especially among mechanics?

Ans. It is.

Ques. State to the Committee what disposition was made of the three ice breakers?

Ans. The first boat built George Spates got—that we built; the second one Sheridan built and Mans got, and the third one, built on the Weld side, is on the Cumberland Division.

Re-Cross-Examination by Mr. Poe.

Ques. When you came into charge of your superintendency, can you tell how many boats, ice breakers and scows, were on the Cumberland Division?

Ans. Two scows; one old one and one pretty good one, and one house boat.

By Mr. Gordon.

Ques. What boats have you built since for that Division?

Ans. One ice breaker in 1867 and one in 1868, one house boat and one small scow for the use of the house boat in 1867.

R. M. SPRIGG.

WILLIAM DOWDEN sworn.

By Mr. Schley.

Ques. Where do you live?

Ans. In South Mechanic street, Cumberland.

Ques. What is your occupation?

Ans. Blacksmith.

Ques. Did you do any work for the canal?

Ans. Yes, sir.

Ques. State to the Committee whether or not you ironed any ice-breakers in the fall of 1867, and if you did, how many, and where they were built?

Ans. I ironed three. Two of them were built down below the shop, and the other was built on the other side of the basin, in Weld's yard.

Cross-Examination by Mr. Gordon.

Ques. Who paid you for ironing them?

Ans. When I went to settle for them Mr, Sprigg said two the Company would pay, and the other he would pay for. I guess there is a voucher for two together.

Ques. What month was that in?

Ans. I cannot say exactly; either in November or December, 1867.

Ques. Was there any other Wm. Dowden besides you working for the Company?

Ans. No, sir. I have a son named Wm. Dowden, but he was not working for the Company.

Ques. How much did you get for ironing an ice breaker?

Ans. Twenty dollars.

By Mr. Schley.

Ques. The Company furnishes all the iron, does it not?

Ans. Yes, sir.

Ques. Who built the other ice breaker on the opposite side, in Weld's yard?

Ans. I do not know what men there were at work on it—there were some five or six.

Ques. Who built the ice breaker on this side?

Ans. Carpenters in the Canal Company's shop. I could not recollect whether they did all the work on it. They might have had extra hands because they wanted them done badly, and I had to work late on Saturday night to get it ready on Sunday morning.

Ques. Did you know of any boat builder in Cumberland by the name of Thomas Sheridan except the man in Mr. Weld's employment of that name?

Ans. No, sir.

Ques. Did you know him?

Ans. I did.

Ques. Did you ever hear of any other boat builder by the name of Thomas Sheridan?

Ans. Not that I recollect of.

Ques. How long had you been working at the Canal Company's wharf?

Ans. I have been working for the Canal Company and keeping lock ever since 1853 or '54.

Ques. How long have you been working where you now are at the wharf or basin?

Ans. I have been there for three years.

Ques. Do not the Canal Company's hands pass by your shop as they go down to the boat yard?

Ans. Yes, sir, but there might be a hundred people passing by and I not know it, as the doors do not face the tow-path.

By Mr. Schley.

Ques. Did I understand you to say you knew all the hands that worked on those boats?

Ans. No, sir.

Ques. Might there not have been another Tom Sheridan working on that boat and you not know it?

Ans. There might have been two or three Tom Sheridans working there and I not know it. I only knew the Company's regular hands. There were other hands working on the boats besides the regular hands.

WM. DOWDEN.

DANIEL WINEOW sworn.

By Mr. Schley.

Ques. Where do you live?

Ans. In Cumberland.

Ques. Were you in the employment of the Chesapeake and Ohio Canal Company, and if so, when?

Ans. I was for three years until within the last two or three months.

Ques. What was your employment?

Ans. Inspector and lock tender on the Cumberland Division, at Cumberland.

Ques. How near is the lock house to the Company's boat yard?

Ans. Within twenty-five yards.

Ques. Are you in the employment of the Canal Company now?

Ans. I am not. I was turned out about the last of November.

Ques. Do you know whether or not any ice breakers were built in 1867, and if so, how many, and where they were built?

Ans. There were three built in the fall of 1867; two were built near the shop, and one was built across the Canal on Mr. Weld's yard.

Ques. How many were built in the Company's yard at one time?

Ans. One was built in the Company's yard and one across on the other side of the basin at the same time. There had been one built in the Company's yard before.

Cross-Examination by Mr. Gordon.

Ques. What hands were at work on those boats that were built on the side next the shop?

Ans. It is hard for me to tell. I do not know.

Ques. How many carpenters had the Company in its employ?
Ans. I do not know.

Ques. Were there any other hands besides the Company's hands?
Ans. Yes, sir.

Ques. Do you know their names?
Ans. I do not. There was a stranger there that they called Sheridan.

Ques. Who did you hear call him Sheridan?
Ans. Several persons. He went by that name.

Ques Was he working just as the other hands?
Ans. I think he was managing the boat.

DANIEL WINEOW.

GEORGE HUGHES sworn.

By Mr. Schley.

Ques. Tell the Committee where you live?
Ans. In Cumberland.

Ques. What is your occupation?
Ans. My occupation is navigating the Chesapeake and Ohio Canal I own boats on it.

Ques. State to the Committee whether or not you have any knowledge of any ice breakers being built at Cumberland in the fall of 1867, and if so, how many were built, and where?
Ans. I have a very distinct knowledge that there were three built in Cumberland—two of them were built on the side the lock stands on, on the Company's yard, and one of them on the opposite side, on the Weld yard.

Ques. State if you know where they went?
Ans. One of them went to Mr. Man's Division, another went to George Spates' Division, to the best of my knowledge, and another was left at Cumberland.

By Mr. Gordon.

Ques. How do you know that fact?
Ans. I understood when the boats were leaving that that was their destination. I cannot be positive as I did not go with them, but that was the rumor.

By Mr. Schley.

Ques. You know that two went away and that one remained?
Ans. Yes.

Ques. State to the Committee when you had two boat loads of corn for Cumberland caught in the ice?

Ans. In the winter of 1867.

Ques. Where were you caught in the ice?

Ans. At Dam No. 5.

Ques. What boat came to help you?

Ans. Mr. Sprigg's boat from the Cumberland Division.

Ques. After you were caught state how you got the ice breaker to come from that Division to another to your assistance?

Ans. I had a way bill from the Company to Cumberland, and I went up and saw Col. Spates, and he directed Mr. Sprigg to take his ice breaker down. The ice was from nine to ten inches thick and that ice breaker broke it, with 45 head of mules attached to it, and enabled me to bring my two loads of corn to Cumberland. I had 25 mules attached to it, but did not charge anything for their helping to break the ice.

By Mr. Gordon.

Ques. Were you caught in 1868?

Ans. My boats came through with less ice. We had to break the ice, but a great deal less stock broke it. To the best of my knowledge it required only nine head.

Ques. Is the ice breaking at the expense of the Canal Company?

Ans. A majority of it, but I made no charge to the Company for furnishing teams, I would rather do it than delay.

GEORGE HUGHES.

WILLIAM WINEOW sworn.

By Mr. Schley.

Ques. State to the Committee where you lived in 1867?

Ans. In the lock house of the Chesapeake and Ohio Canal at Cumberland.

Ques. State to the Committee whether or not any ice breakers were built in Cumberland in 1867, and if so, how many were built and where they were built?

Ans. There were three built that I know of, two of them at the Canal Company's shop, and one opposite the Canal Company's shop in Weld's yard.

Ques. Were there two building at the same time on the Canal Company's ground?

Ans. No, sir.

Ques. Do you know where those boats went?

Ans. I do not.

Ques. Do you know whether or not any of them were sent away?
Ans. Two of them were sent away.

WM. WINEOW.

Mr. Schley offered in evidence an abstract of R. M. Sprigg, Cumberland Division, Nov. 1867, the entry, "two ice breakers, $1,300." Also, on abstract of I. R. Mans, Georgetown Division, Nov. 1867, the entry, " No. 83, Thomas Sheridan, $800." Also Thomas Sheridan's receipt for $800.

GEORGE W. SPATES sworn.

Ques. Where do you live?
Ans. In Montgomery county.

Ques. Were you in the employment of the Canal Company in 1867?
Ans. I have been ever since 1862.

Ques. In what position?
Ans. Superintendent of the Seneca Division.

Ques. Did you in the fall of 1867 receive an ice breaker from Cumberland?
Ans. I did.

Ques. Did you made any charge for it on your abstract for Nov. 1867?
Ans. I do not know. I do not think I did.

Ques. Did you pay any money for it?
Ans. As my memory serves me I do not think I did.

Ques. Was it furnished from your Division, or from the Cumberland Division?
Ans. From the Cumberland Division. I went to Cumberland after it in November, 1867.

Cross-examination by Mr. Gordon.

Ques. How many ice-breakers had you on your Division in 1867?
Ans. Two.

Ques. Did this new one make three?
Ans. One of the old ones rotted out and I had but one when I got the new one. I then had but two.

Ques. How many are there now on that Division?
Ans. Two.

Re-Examination by Mr. Schley.

Ques. Are you Superintendent of the Seneca Division now?
Ans. No.

Ques. When were you displaced?

Ans. I resigned sometime about the first of December.

Ques. Was or was not there any propositions made to you, and if so, by whom, of the terms upon which you could retain your position?

Ans. There were two or three propositions made to me by those two gentlemen.

Mr. Poe.

By what two gentlemen?
Ans. By you and Mr. Gordon.

By Mr. Schley.

Ques. State what those propositions were?

Ans. Mr. Poe and Mr. Gordon were together on the packet, and sent for me to meet the Board at the head of my Division. When I got on board they invited me into a little room and commenced rolling out a lot of papers, and Mr. Gordon came up and sat down by me, and said, "tell us, did you not pay that money to the President?" pointing to Tasker's account, and said I, " I paid all the money on my account to whatever names are on the abstract."

Ques. What other conversation did you have?

Ans. I had a conversation with Mr. Poe prior to that, in front of the City Hotel, in Frederick. I approached him and said, "Mr. Poe, I understand I am to be turned out," and he said, "whenever you do right, and do what this Board wants you to do, you need not fear being turned out."

Mr. Poe.

Ques. Is that what you call a proposition?
Ans. That is what I understood as a proposition.

By Mr. Schley.

Ques. What did you understand him to mean?

Ans. I understood from that that I was to do whatever they wanted me to do, to agree to anything, or say anything, or do anything they wanted.

Ques. When did that meeting take place?

Ans. Prior to the meeting on the packet—in October. The meeting on the packet took place in November.

Ques. Take your abstract for November, 1867, and see whether you made any charge on it for an ice breaker you received from the Cumberland Division in November, 1867?

Ans. I cannot see any. I find none there.

Mr. Poe.—It is due to Mr. Spates that I should state, that the conversation which he relates as having taken place between himself and me is, with some slight variation, nearly correct. I do not know that it will be necessary for me to put myself on the stand as a witness, but will say that it is quite well known among the employees of the canal that I was in the Board in rather exceptional attitude, and from rumor it became known that I was opposed to the removal of any officer except upon charges. This gentleman approached me at the door of the hotel and said, Mr. Poe, I hope I am not to be turned out. I think I asked him who he was. He explained to me, and I said he would not be turned out by my vote, for I never had voted for the removal of any officer if he did his duty.

Mr. Gordon.

Ques. What did Mr. Thompson say?

Ans. "Your explanation of what you did with the money is not satisfactory. We are going to turn you out, and unless you give a better one we are going to sue you."

GEO. W. SPATES.

NOS. 2 & 3.

SATURDAY, March 12, 1870.

The Committee met at 9 o'clock, A. M.

Present as before.

Mr. Schley offered in evidence "Proceedings of the President and Directors," Nov. 5th, 1868, page 119, which is as follows:

"The Clerk laid before the Board the following estimates of Super-"intendent for the October expenses:

"R. M. Sprigg, Cumberland Division...............................	$4,500
"Denton Jaques, Hancock...	2,250
"Jacob B. Masters, Williamsport.....................................	1,950
"John Shay, Antietam..	2,500
"Amos Thomas, Monocacy...	1,700
"Geo. W. Spates, Seneca..	3,100
"Isaac R. Mans, Georgetown...	2,950
	$18,950

"Which were severally approved and the Treasurer ordered to draw "checks for the same."

Present at that meeting Alfred Spates, President, and Joseph Murray, A. K. Stake, Jno. B. Thomas, W. Veirs Bouic and Esau Pickerell, Directors.

Mr. Schley also offered in evidence Abstract of John Shay for October, 1868, and entry in amounts paid to various parties on that Abstract—J. J. Bruce, $652.60. Also receipt of John J. Bruce for $652.60.

RICHARD M. SPRIGG recalled.

By Mr. Schley.

Ques. State to the Committee whether, or not, in the fall of 1868, Mr. Spates called upon you to go with him to Dr. Bruce's to pay him for the lumber for the Antietam and Georgetown Divisions, gotten by Shay and Mans.

Ans. He did.

Ques. Where were you at the time he called on you?

Ans. Down at the Canal lock.

Ques. What were you doing there?

Ans. Settling with the hands.

Ques. Did you, or not, then go with Mr. Spates to Dr. Bruce's office at his lumber yard?

Ans. I did.

Ques. What took place at the time you went with Mr. Spates to Dr. Bruce's office?

Ans. Mr. Spates came to me at the Canal lock and told me he had been looking for me, he wanted me to go with him to Dr. Bruce's, that he wanted to pay for some lumber bought for the Shay and Mans boats. I walked into the office when we got there and, and said I, "Doctor, Col. Spates has come to pay his bill. Is there any of that lumber in my bill." "No," said he, "not a stick of it." Said I, "make out your bill, and Colonel Spates is here ready to pay you." He made out the two bills and counted it up, and it amounted to $1,052.60. Mr. Spates pulled out a roll of money from his pantaloons pocket, and commenced counting it up, and was so long at it that I remarked I could have counted $4,000 in the same time. The amount he paid was $1,052.60, and I remember that Mr. Spates gave me a dollar and I gave him the change so as to make the sixty cents.

Ques. Look at the two bills—the Mans and Shay bills—and see if they make up that amount?

Ans. They do make up that amount, $1,052.60, and are in Dr. Bruce's handwriting.

Ques. Did you see Dr. Bruce give Col. Spates a receipt for that money?

Ans. I did.

Mr. Schley offered in evidence resolution on page 105, " Proceedings of the President and Directors Chesapeake and Ohio Canal Company," adopted at the meeting of the Board, August 13, 1868. Present, Alfred Spates, President, and Joseph Murray, A. K. Stake, W. Veirs Bouic, George Colton, and Esau Pickerell, Directors.

" On motion, it was ordered that the President and General Superintendent have a new scow built for the use of the Georgetown Division, also a scow and house boat for Seneca Division."

Mr. Schley also offered in evidence entry on Abstract of Isaac R. Mans, for October, 1868, " No. 57, John J. Bruce, $400." Also receipt of Jno. J. Bruce for $400, dated Nov. 9th, 1868."

Cross-Examination by Mr. Gordon.

Ques. Look at that paper marked J. J. Bruces' receipt for $1,257.10. Did you file that as a voucher with your abstract?

Ans. I did.

Ques. Did you pay that money?

Ans. I did.

Ques. To whom?

Ans. To Dr. Bruce.

Ques. When did you pay it?

Ans. On the 9th of November.

Ques. What was that for?

Ans. For various purposes. I was not a mechanic, and do not know what it went into. I made my report to you. The receipt was returned as a voucher in my abstract for October.

Ques. Is that the abstract you returned, (marked R. M. Sprigg's abstract for Oct., 1868?)

Ans. It is.

Ques. Is it made out by you in your handwriting?

Ans. No, sir. It was made out by Mr. Lowe, my clerk, and I authorized Mr. Lowe to sign it for me.

Ques. Was this paper pasted on it when you filed it in the office?

Ans. It was. I put it on after Mr. Lowe gave it to me. I saw he had made out the summary wrong, and I pasted this paper over it.

Ques. Is that in your handwriting?

Ans. No, sir.

Ques. What was written under that?

Ans. I do not recollect now, but know the summary was not made out in the way I wanted it.

Ques. Did you pay this $1,257.10 to Dr. Bruce in addition to what Col. Spates paid to Dr. Bruce on the Shay and Mans' account?

Ans. Yes, sir; that was my own bill.

Ques. Who was with you when you paid this?

Ans. Nobody at all.

Ques. Was anybody present besides you and Dr. Bruce when you paid it?

Ans. I do not think there was.

Ques. You got an allowance for this $1,257.10 bill in you abstract?

Ans. Yes, sir; I was paid the money on it.

Ques. Are these receipts all made out in your handwriting, except the signature of Sheridan?

Ans. They are. I filled them up and Sheridan witnessed them, and I paid the money at the time.

Ques. Were the men in the office at the time?

Ans. They were not; they were out at work.

Ques. Did not these men write their names?

Ans. I do not know. I did not ask them. Sheridan told me to fill them up and he would sign them.

Ques. You returned those as your vouchers, did you?

Ans. Yes, sir. That was the understanding when I got the men, that I was to pay the money to him. I was to pay him the same as we paid our hands, $2.25, and a bonus of fifty cents apiece a day to him, making $2.75. We were glad to get his hands at any price at that time.

Ques. How much did you pay to Mr. Sheridan at that time?

Ans. The amount of those receipts.

Ques. Was there anything else?

Ans. I think there was some oakum. I do not recollect all his bill called for. I have never looked at those receipts since I filed them away.

Ques. In regard to this abstract, will you be kind enough to state what the list on the second page is for?

Ans. That is the time of the laborers, other than the mechanics.

Ques. How did you get that time?

Ans. I got that time from the bosses, and returned it in my abstract as the bosses returned it to me. I never kept the time of any of the men except one man. Some of the receipts on the time-book are a few days short. The difference is accounted for by having included in the time of the men small bills for railroad fare, &c., which was done by your direction.

Ques. Did you allow any time for contingencies in those bills of Sheridan's?

Ans. I did not.

Ques. Who was the one man you spoke of whose time you kept?

Ans. Nicholas Furlong. We had him employed watch to keep people from stealing lumber and burning the shop down. I had suspected persons of trying to burn the shop down, and a great deal of lumber had been stolen. He was employed at the bank at night. We employed him in the day time, and he was to be on guard as much as he could at night.

Ques. How long was he employed by you?

Ans. I do not recollect; but he was there from the time I first got him until a month before I was turned off the Canal.

R. M. SPRIGG.

Mr. Schley offered in evidence endorsement on abstract of R. M. Sprigg for October, 1868, "Examined and approved January 29, 1869, John B. Thomas and Esau Pickerell, Committee on Accounts;" also, report of the Committee on Accounts to the Board, adopted February 4th, 1869, pp. 134 and 135, as follows:

"The Committee on Accounts report that they have examined the following accounts, for which vouchers have been exhibited, to wit:" * * *

4. The accounts of Isaac R. Mans, Superintendent of the Georgetown Division, from June 1st, 1868, to December 31st, '68.

5. The accounts of George W. Spates, Superintendent of the Seneca Division, from August 1st, 1868, to December 31st, 1868.

6. The accounts of George W. Spates, Superintendent of the Monocacy Division, from June 1st, 1868, to July 31st, 1868.

7. The accounts of Amos Thomas, Superintendent of Monocacy Division, from August 1st, 1868, to December 31st, 1868.

8. The accounts of John Shay, Superintendent of Antietam Division, from 1st of June, 1868, to 31st of December, 1868.

11. The accounts of R. M. Sprigg, Superintendent of Cumberland Division, from June 1st, 1868, to 31st of December, 1868.

* * The Committee, in conclusion, recommend that all the accounts examined be passed upon and approved by the Board, "signed John B. Thomas and Esau Pickerell, Committee on Accounts;" also, resolution passed by the full Board, Dec. 3d, 1868, p. 122, "Journal of Proceedings," as follows:

"On motion, the following resolution was adopted:

"*Resolved*, That in addition to the foregoing repairs, the General Superintendent cause all such other repairs to be done as may be found to be necessary and proper to put the Canal from Washington city to Cumberland in good and permanent navigable order for the ensuing year, and to pay the cost thereof, the sum of one hundred thousand dollars ($100,000) be and the same is hereby appropriated, to be paid from time to time, as may be specially ordered by the Board, upon the report of the repairs, as made by the several Superintendents and approved by the General Superintendent and by the Board."

Also, resolution passed by the Board September 26th, 1867, page 48, "Proceedings, &c."

"*Resolved,* That Alfred Spates be authorized and requested to give "his personal attention and supervision over the employees of the Com- "pany along the line, and over the entire line of the Canal, and to "exercise all the duties of *General Superintendent* of the Canal, with "power to remove all persons along the line, and to fill their places "whenever the interests of the Company demands it, subject to the ap- "proval or disapproval of this Board."

Also, "By-Laws, Rules and Regulations of the Chesapeake and Ohio Canal Company," page 34, as follows:

"The General Superintendent shall have the general management and direction of all repairs and improvements of the canal that may, from time to time, be required. He shall give general directions and instructions to the superintendents of repairs in regard to the manner of making and carrying on the ordinary repairs, and special directions and instructions in regard to all those not of an ordinary character, and in regard to all improvements.

" He shall, so far as practicable, personally examine all breaches, particularly those that will take more than one week for their repair, and shall give special directions and instructions to the superintendents of repairs in regard to the manner in which they shall be repaired.

" He shall, as often as practicable, examine the accounts of the super- intendents of repairs, to ascertain whether economy is observed in the doing of the work entrusted to their management; and may, if he think it advisable, at any time, require that their accounts and vouchers for disbursements shall be transmitted, through him, to the canal office.

" He may, if he think it advisable, require that all reports and re- turns made by any or all of the superintendents of repairs to the office of the Company shall be transmitted through him; and in like man- ner that all communications to them from the office of the Company shall be transmitted through him.

" He may, if he deem it necessary, suspend any superintendent or lock keeper, and fill the vacancy thereby created until the next meeting of the President and Directors, at which time he shall report to the said President and Directors such suspension and temporary appointment, with his reasons therefor and the facts of the case."

CHARGE No. 4.

Tuesday, March 15th, 1870.

The Committee met at 4 o'clock P. M., pursuant to adjournment. Present as before.

Mr. Schley offered in evidence "Proceedings of the President and and Directors," August 13, 1868, page 105, the following resolution adopted by the President and five Directors:

"On motion, it was ordered that the President and General Super-"intendent have a new scow built for the use of the Georgetown Divi-"sion, also a scow and house boat for Seneca Division."

R. M. Sprigg recalled.

By Mr. Schley.

Ques. State to the Committee whether or not, in the fall of 1868, a scow or ice breaker and house boat were built in Cumberland for Seneca Division, of which George W. Spates was Superintendent?

Ans. Yes.

Ques. Do you know for whom they were built?

Ans. For George W. Spates. He came there and took them both away himself.

Mr. Schley also offered in evidence "Proceedings of the President and Directors," January 7, 1869, page 126:

"Reports were read from the Superintendents of Georgetown, Seneca, "Monocacy, Antietam, Williamsport, Hancock and Cumberland Divisions.

"On motion of Judge Bouic, the report of R. M. Sprigg, Superin-"tendent of the Cumberland Division, was referred to the Committee "on Accounts of this Board."

Ques. Did you make a report to the Board?

Ans. Yes, sir.

Mr. Schley also offered "Proceedings, &c.," February 4th, 1869, (present the President and five Directors,) pages 134 and 135:

"The Committee on Accounts report to the Board that they have examined the following accounts, for which vouchers have been exhibited to wit:

* * * * * * * *

"*Fourth*—The accounts of Isaac R. Mans, Superintendent of Georgetown Division, from June 1st, 1868, to 31st December, 1868.

"*Fifth*.—The accounts of George W. Spates, Superintendent of Seneca Division, from August 1st, 1868, to 31st December, 1868.

"*Sixth*.—The accounts of George W. Spates, Superintendent of Monocacy Division, from June 1st, 1868, to 31st July, 1868.

* * * * * * * *

"*Eighth*.—The accounts of John Shay, Superintendent of Antietam Division, from June 1st, 1868, to 31st December, 1868.

* * * * * * * *

"*Eleventh*.—The accounts of R. M. Sprigg, Superintendent of Cumberland Division, from June 1st, 1868, to 31st December, 1868"

Ques. Look at the paper now shown to you, (marked report of R. M. Sprigg, December 31st, 1868,) and state whether it is the report you made to the President and Directors of the Chesapeake and Ohio Canal Company; whether it is your signature, and what months it embraces?

Ans. That is my signature, and this is the report made by me for lumber used in my Division for the months of August, September, October and November, 1868. I think I have never seen the report since I sent it in.

Ques. What do you set forth in that report?

Ans. Where I used the lumber bought for the Cumberland Division during those months.

Ques. Does that embrace all the lumber you bought and used on the Cumberland Division for those four months?

Ans. I think it does. There may be some little I overlooked.

Ques. When you sent that report to the Canal Board were there or not any papers accompanying that report, and if so, state what papers they were?

Ans. I sent with the report duplicates of two bills and receipts of Tasker & Co.'s and of two bills and receipts of Dr. Bruce's.

Ques. Do you know in whose handwriting those duplicates are?

Ans. I do not know. I think they are in Patterson's handwriting, but will not be certain.

Ques. Who handed you those duplicates to Tasker & Co.'s two bills and Dr. Bruce's two bills?

Ans. Col. Spates.

Ques. Was not Col. Spates with you when you went into Tasker & Co.'s establishment, on Baltimore street, to pay him a bill of $209, due by the Canal Company?

Ans. He was. He joined me on the street and walked up there with me.

Ques. State to the Committee what happened when you went in to pay Tasker that bill?

Ques. I walked in first and Mr. Spates after me. I told Mr. McCulley I had come to pay the bill the Canal Company owed him. He made out the bill and I paid him the money. Mr. Spates was standing behind me at the time. As soon as I paid the bill we walked out and went up to Mr. Gephart's foundry.

Ques. Why did you go there?

Ans. Mr. Spates wanted to pay for some castings gotten for Shay.

Ques. Was there or not any difficulty at the time you paid that bill to McCulley?

Ans. None at all.

Ques. Did you hear Col. Spates make any remark?

Ans. Not a word

Ques. Where was Tasker standing at the time you were paying McCulley that bill?

Ans. Off at one end of the store, near the door. I was standing to the left of Mr. McCulley, and Mr. Spates was standing behind me.

Ques Did or did not Tasker hand two billheads to Col. Spates and say to him, "As we cannot arrange the bill to suit you, you can take those and make them out to suit yourself?"

Ans. I never heard a word of that mentioned.

Ques. State whether or not you had a conversation with Ezekiel Male in regard to some car loads of lumber for the Canal Company from Tasker & Co.'s, and as near as you can recollect, who was with you at the time and where it took place?

Ans. Two weeks ago yesterday, on Monday, the last day of February, Mr. Spates and I had been down to Brengle's, and we were walking up and Zeke Male passed by on the opposite side of the street. I remarked, "There goes Zeke Male," and called him over and asked him if he recollected having received the lumber the Canal Company got from Tasker & Co. He said all the lumber he had anything to do with was in the yard, but there were three car loads and a half of lumber standing on the track, above the depot, directed to the Canal Company, and he did not know whether the Canal Company had taken the half away, but when he saw it there were three and a half car loads standing there. Mr. Spates asked him if anybody else got lumber in that way. He said yes, whenever it was sold by the car load it was measured at the mill.

Ques. Did you or not pay for any of the lumber that went into the ice breaker and house boat of George Spates except what is in this report?

Ans. No, sir; not a foot of it.

Ques. Did you or not pay for any of the lumber that went into the Shay and Mans boats except what is set forth in that report?

Ans. The match stuff—the flooring and ceiling of the cabins—is all I paid for.

Cross-Examination by Mr. Gordon.

Ques. Did not you make a monthly report to the Board of what you had done during the month?

Ans. All the report I made was the abstract.

Ques. Do not your abstracts show all the materials which you buy during the month?

Ans. Sometimes they do and sometimes they do not.

Ques. Is not that the object of them?

Ans. Yes, sir.

Ques. Had you made a report for each of those months?

Ans. I had.

Ques. How did you come to make this extra report?

Ans. By direction of the Board.

Ques. Were you at the Board?

Ans. No, sir. I was not.

Ques. How did you know that the Board directed you to make it?

Ans. I had a written order from the Board to make it.

Ques. From whom did you get it?

Ans. I do not recollect.

Ques. Did you ever see your reports for September and October after they were filed in the Canal office?

Ans. No, sir.

Ques. Did I understand you to say those pieces of paper were pasted on them when they were filed in the office?

Ans. Yes, sir.

Ques. Were they not brought to you afterwards?

Ans. No, sir. I never saw them after I sent them to the office.

Ques. Did you get the money represented in your abstracts for August, September, October and November?

Ans. Yes, sir.

Ques. You state in this report: "In my return for the month of "September of this year I estimated the building of two of these boats "at $800.00 each—one to the Seneca Division, and one to the Antietam "Division—and lumber for the house boat for Seneca Division at "$300.00; this was an error which I beg leave to correct, as I under- "stood at first the order for the building of these boats to be that I was "to use the lumber then on hand." You had lumber then on hand?

Ans. We kept a surplus of lumber always on hand?

Ques. Where did you correct that error, or did you correct it, and how?

Ans. I corrected it by putting on that piece of paper, which showed where the lumber went.

Ques. You got the money for that month did you?

Ans. I did.

Ques. You say here that "no part of those boats were built in August or September, nor was any part of the lumber purchased in August, September, October or November, used in the construction of them except as hereinbefore stated," is that correct?

Ans. It is. The statement as to where the lumber is comes before that part.

Ques. Where is Lock 69?
Ans. The lower lock at Old Town.

Ques. Who kept that lock?
Ans. Dennison is there now.

Ques. You built a new lock house there did you?
Ans. Yes, sir.

Ques. When did you build it?
Ans. In 1867.

Ques. Did you build any other lock house at Old Town?
Ans. No.

Ques. Did you repair any other lock house at Old Town?
Ans. Yes. We repaired both of them some.

Ques, Whose handwriting is this report in?
Ans. John Patterson. I got him to copy it from one I made out.

Ques. How much lumber had you on hand at that time?
Ans. I cannot tell you that. We always kept a good deal of lumber on hand of all kinds, for building boats and everything else we needed.

Ques. Do you say that these receipts of Bruce's and Tasker's were sent in with this report?
Ans. I could not say that they are the ones, but I sent in receipts similar to them copied in Patterson's handwriting. I asked for them to enable me to make up my report.

Ques. Did you get them from Mr. Spates?
Ans. He got them for me. I asked him for them several days before I got them.

By Mr. Schley.

Ques. When were these boats for George Spates built?
Ans. In October and November.

Ques. Were there any more boats built in October and November, and if so, for whom were they built?

Ans. Yes; we had five going at the same time. We got the lumber at one time for all of them. We had a bottom of a house boat for Mans, and we had an ice breaker for Shay, a breaker for George Spates, and one for the Cumberland Division.

R. M. SPRIGG.

FRANCIS SMELTZER sworn.

By Mr. Schley.

Ques. Where do you live?
Ans. In Cumberland.

Ques. What is your occupation?
Ans. Carpenter.

Ques. State whether or not you have been in the employment of the Chesapeake and Ohio Canal Company, and if so, how long?

Ans. I commenced working for the Company on the 14th day of December, 1866, and have been with them ever since until last Friday evening, when I left to come here.

Ques. Do you not know of the building of boats of various kinds at Cumberland in the fall of 1868?
Ans. Yes, sir.

Ques. Do you know whether there were boats built there at that time for Shay, Mans and George Spates?

Ans. I cannot say anything about the Shay and Mans boats, but know that George Spates came there and got two of the boats. The other boats went away, but I do not know where they went.

Ques. How many boats were built at Cumberland in the fall of 1868?
Ans. One house boat and three ice breakers.

Ques. Was there not also a bottom of a house boat or scow built?
Ans. Yes; there was.

Ques. Did you or not work on the Geo. Spates boats?
Ans. I did.

Ques. Where did the lumber come from that went into those boats?
Ans. From Tasker & Co.

Ques. Did you or not help to unload car loads of lumber from Tasker & Co's. for the Geo. Spates boats, and if so, how many.

Ans. I did. There were four cars that had lumber on. The siding was 60 feet long, and it would not lie on one car. The light lumber was piled along with the other lumber.

Ques. Did you help to work that stuff into the Geo. Spates boats?
Ans. I did. Both into the ice breaker and the house boat.

Cross-Examination by Mr. Gordon.

Ques. How much lumber was there on each car?
Ans. That is more than I am able to say. I had no way of measuring it.

Ques. How many thousand feet would a car hold? As many as two thousand?

Ans. That is more than I would be able to say. I would suppose something near ten thousand.

Ques. How do you know that lumber came from Tasker & Co's.?

Ans. Because Berston told me that there was lumber from Tasker & Co.'s up at the depot, and told me where the cars stood, and because Evans was out there two or three times helping to unload it.

Ques. What was lumber worth a thousand?
Ans. I do not know.

Ques. Was it worth as much as $100 a thousand?
Ans. I do not know what they charge for lumber of that kind.

Ques. How did those sides come?
Ans. On the cars.

Ques. What sort of cars?
Ans. Gondolas.

By Mr. Schley.

Ques. Evans was the clerk of Tasker & Co., wasn't he?
Ans. Yes.

Ques. Did you or not commence working on those boats when they were commenced and continue on them till finished?
Ans. I did.

Ques. State whether, or not, all the lumber that went into those boats, except the flooring and ceiling, did not come from Tasker & Co's.?

Ans. All the lumber that went into the George Spates' ice breaker and house boat, came from there, with the exception of the match lumber, and that came from Bruce's.

FRANCIS SMELTZER.

JAMES NOOMAN sworn.

By Mr. Schley.

Ques. Where do you live?
Ans. In Cumberland.

Ques. What is your occupation?
Ans. Carpenter.

Ques. Where have you been working at your trade?
Ans. With the Canal Company.

Ques. How long?
Ans. Six years.

Ques. Do you, or not, recollect whether you helped to unload, or to haul any lumber from the depot that came from Tasker & Co's. to the Canal Company?

Ans. I did.

Ques. Have you any recollection of the number of car loads you helped to unload?

Ans. I could not tell. I helped to unload it from the wagons in the yard.

Ques. Did you work on the boats built for George W. Spates?

Ans. Yes.

Ques. What lumber did you work into those boats?

Ans. The lumber I got from Mr. Tasker's.

Cross-Examination—by Mr. Gordon.

Ques. Where did you see the lumber?

Ans. In the yard.

Ques. Do you know anything about where it came from?

Ans. Tasker & Co's.

Ques. How do you know?

Ans. Because his drivers were hauling it.

Ques. Who were his drivers?

Ans. Paddy Lynch, Jimmy Monohen and Male.

JAMES NOONAN.

WILLIAM WINEOW recalled.

By Mr. Schley.

Ques. Where do yo you live?

Ans. In Cumberland.

Ques. What is your occupation?

Ans. At present I am working at the carpenters' trade.

Ques. Were you not working for the Chesapeake and Ohio Canal in the fall of 1868?

Ans. I was.

Ques. Did you not work on the boats built for George W. Spates?

Ans. I dio.

Ques. Do you know where the lumber came from that went into those boats?

Ans. I know by what Berston told me—

Mr. Gordon—Do not state what you heard from others. That is not evidence.

Ques. Did you not see lumber at the depot?

Ans. I passed there one day and saw Smeltzer unloading lumber from the cars, and understood it came from Tasker & Co's.

By Mr. Gordon.

Ques. What is lumber worth a thousand?

Ans. That I cannot tell you.

CLEMENT A. PECK sworn.

By Mr. Schley.

Ques. Have you been at any time employed in the office of the Canal Company, and, if so, in what capacity?

Ans. I was assistant clerk in the office until the 1st of last October. I went into their employment on the 1st of July, 1860.

Ques. Had you or not under your charge the abstracts of the Superintendents of the various Divisions?

Ans. Yes, sir; I examined them.

Ques. Look at the abstract of George W. Spates for November, 1868, and see whether that came into the office whilst you were there?

Ans. It did.

Ques. What are the charges entered there in Tasker's name?

Ans. H. P. Tasker & Co. $1,200, and H. P. Tasker & Co. $150.

Ques. Have you any recollection of vouchers for those amounts?

Ans. I presume there were vouchers for those amounts. It sometimes occurred that the vouchers were not with the abstracts, and the Superintendents supplied them afterwards. If they were not there at the time, I generally made a note and wrote to them. I see none on these. The vouchers must have been supplied.

Ques. Do you remember ever putting a mark on the vouchers by which you could recognize them?

Ans. I do not.

Ques. Take the two receipts of H. P. Tasker, for $1,200 and $150, and look at the head of them, and state whether the words "Voucher No. 54," and "Voucher No. 55," are in your handwriting?

Ans. No, sir. It sometimes happens that the vouchers are not numbered, and I generally put the number on them in red ink, but do not remember ever writing "Voucher." The writing does not look like mine, and I feel very certain it is not.

Ques. Do you, or not, recollect anything in regard to the Tasker vouchers, as to whether the body of the bill was in one ink and the signature in another?

Ans. My impression is that they were made out in a different hand from the one in which they were signed, but I do not feel certain about that.

Ques. Before the office was removed from Washington to this place had you charge of the effects there?

Ans. I had charge of one room, where the books were kept. There were four or five rooms rented to the Company.

Ques. Do you know whether a piece of furniture was sent from the President's room to Mr. Grove?

Ans. No, sir; not out of that room. There was a desk up stairs that was taken out while I was there, and put into a wagon and sent over to Georgetown. I understood it was for Mr. Grove; I was told so.

By Mr. Gordon.

Ques. Who told you so?

Ans. Mr. Fawcett. The driver charged one dollar for taking it over, and Mr. Grove was to pay for that. That was in September. The office was not moved until December.

Cross-Examination by Mr. Poe.

Ques. You say the words "Voucher No. 54" and "Voucher No. 55" are not in your handwriting. State whether or not, in your opinion, they are in the handwriting of George W. Spates?

Ans. I do not know.

Ques. Do not the Superintendents always number their vouchers?

Ans. They do. It is an omission when they do not.

Ques. Are the figures 54 and 55 on the abstract made by you or somebody else?

Ans. They are not made by me.

Ques. Are they made by the same person that made the figures on the vouchers?

Ans. I am unable to say. They look something alike.

By Mr. Schley.

Ques. Do you, or not, recollect any conversation you had with Fawcett in regard to whether or not this was a fight between Col. Spates and himself, and, if so, state what it was?

Ans. Mr. Fawcett did not often talk to me about those things, but when he did he generally did it confidentially. He did not tell me, but think he told me he had told a Director it was a fight between him and the Board, or the President of the Board, and he would be turned out or would get them out.

By Mr. Poe.

Ques. Have you any recollection of the monthly abstracts of the Superintendent of the Cumberland Division having been taken out of the office at any time by anybody for the purpose of being corrected or altered, after they had been filed in the office?

Ans. I do not know that anybody took them out for that purpose. Sometimes they would be taken by the President and sometimes by some member of the Board.

Ques. Do you recollect whether this particular abstract of Sprigg's for October, 1868, was taken away and returned with that part pasted over it?

Ans. I recollect that Mr. Spates called on me once and asked me to let him look at these abstracts—some three or four of them. He was in the habit of looking at them. I do not know whether he took them away or not, nor do I know exactly when he gave them to me again.

Ques. Can you give any idea how long the abstract was out of your possession?

Ans. I cannot. I hardly think it was a week. It might not have been two days.

Ques. Was the piece of paper pasted on whilst out of your possession?

Ans. I think it was, but it was in the condition it now is when it was examined by the Committee on Accounts.

Ques. Could you tell by inspecting it what is the difference between the writing as it now stands and what it was before it was altered?

Ans. My impression is there is no material difference, the amount is the same.

By Mr. Clarke.

Ques. Is it anything unusual for the President or Directors to come in and ask for papers?

Ans. Not at all. It was a very common thing for the President or Directors to come and get some of those abstracts and carry them up stairs.

Ques. Do not the Board have the abstracts before them when they appropriated money called for by the abstracts?

Ans. No, sir. It was the custom for the Superintendent to tell the Clerk he wanted so much money to pay his expenses and the Clerk would send him the money before it was appropriated by the Board?

By Mr. Schley.

Ques. Did not they in later times make an estimate of what they would want for their expenses, and was not the check drawn in accordance with that estimate?

Ans. It was an old rule that the Superintendent should make out an estimate of what he wanted and the purposes, and then it would come before the Board, but it had not been observed until the last year before I left. It used to be the custom when Mr. Ringold was Clerk and Treasurer for the President to sign blank checks, to be filled up by the Clerk.

By Mr. Gordon.

Ques. Was not that the custom when I came into office?

Ans. I do not think it was. In 1860 it was the custom.

CLEMENT A. PECK.

GEO. W. SPATES recalled.

By Mr. Schley.

Ques. What Division did you Superintend in November, 1868?

Ans. Seneca Division.

Ques. Look at the paper (marked abstract of G. W. Spates for Nov., 1868) and state whether it is the one you filed at the office in November, 1868?

Ans. It is.

Ques. Did your or not pay all that that abstract claims?

Ans. I did.

Ques. Did you or not send vouchers with that abstract, for all those charges to various parties?

Ans. I did.

Ques. Look at the papers (marked receipt of H. P. Tasker & Co., $1,200, and receipt of H. P. Tasker & Co., $150) and state whether you filed those as vouchers with your abstract in November, 1868?

Ans. No, sir. I did not file them.

Ques. When was the first time you saw those two papers and in whose hands were they?

Ans. The first time I recollect seeing them they were in Mr. Poe's hands on board the packet last November.

Ques. Look at the top of them and state whether the words there written "voucher No. 54" and "voucher No. 55" are in your handwriting?

Ans. They are not.

Ques. Did you get an ice breaker and a house boat from Cumberland in 1868?

Ans. I did.

Ques. Did you take them to your Division?

Ans. I did.

Ques. When you went to Cumberland did you or not pay to Tasker & Co. one bill of $1,200, and another of $150?

Ans. I did, and got receipts for them.

Ques. How did you first receive those bills?

Ans. They were sent to me by mail.

Ques. State to the Committee whether or not the body of the bill was not in one handwriting and the receipt in another?

Ans. That is my recollection of it. The ink was not the same in the receipt as in the body of the bill.

Ques. State whether or not you had any conversation with the President of the Canal Company with reference to these Tasker bills, and if so, state that conversation?

Ans. He asked me for copies of those bills to be filed with Mr. Sprigg's report. I told him I did not have copies, but would go and get them from the office. I went there, but they said they had no time to make copies, but would give me the billheads to have copies made. They gave me the billheads, and I gave them to Col. Spates, and he afterwards returned me the original bills to me, and I filed them with my account.

Mr. Schley gave notice that he would require those original bills to be produced which had been filed with the account of G. W. Spates.

Cross-Examined by Mr. Poe.

Ques. Do you recollect at what time in November you came on board the packet?

Ans. About the last of November, 1869.

Ques. Who were present at the conversation which you stated took place at that time?

Ans. You, Mr. Gordon and myself. Mr. Thompson came to the door once and then went away.

Ques. Were you asked by me then whether or not you had paid the money represented by that voucher of $1,200 in Cumberland?

Ans. Yes, and I told you I had paid it to somebody representing the firm of H. P. Tasker & Co., but would not know him if I was to see him now.

Ques. Were you asked where you had paid it?

Ans. I was, and told you I did not know where I had paid it. I think, upon reflection, I paid it in the office of the firm.

Ques. Were you asked who bought the lumber charged in that bill?

Ans. I think you did, and that I told you I did not know, but that I did not buy it.

Ques. Were you asked if the bill had been sent to you in a letter?

Ans. I was, and told you it was sent to me unreceipted, and receipted when I went to Cumberland and paid for it.

Ques. Have you seen Tasker since?

Ans. I would not know Tasker if I was to see him now. I saw somebody here they called Mr. Tasker, but he is not the man to whom I paid the money.

Ques. Do you know Mr. McCulley?

Ans. I do not.

Ques. Did you ask the name of the man to whom you paid the money?

Ans. I did not. I have paid many bills without taking the liberty of asking the names of those to whom I paid them.

Ques. Did you pay the $150 bill at the time you paid the $1,200 bill?

Ans. About the same time. Probably one on one day and one the next.

Ques. State whether when I exhibited to you the $1,200 bill, you said anything about it not being the paper you filed?

Ans. I did not say it was or was not the paper. I told you then I did not think it was the paper.

Ques. Did you not promise to meet the Committee at the office in Washington the next day?

Ans. No. My wife was very sick, and I told you I could not go.

Ques. Did you make an appointment to meet Mr. Thompson and me at Rockville upon another occasion?

Ans. I did not.

By Mr. Schley.

Ques. Did you not pay the $1,200 on November 9, and the $150 bill on November 18?

Ans. I did.

Ques. Did you not buy the lumber in the $150 bill?

Ans. I did, and took it down on my Division to repair locks, to make bridges, and whatever else.

GEO. W. SPATES.

Mr. Gordon asked that John Patterson be again summoned for rebutting evidence, but the Committee decided that since he had been examined and cross-examined, and discharged by consent of both sides, he could not be again summoned.*

---

*NOTE BY COMMITTEE. John Patterson being the only witness for whom a re-summons was desired at this time, the Committee not being satisfied of the materiality of his testimony, declined to order him to be summoned again after he had been discharged, as stated above. He was re-summoned afterwards with other witnesses, by order of the Committee, and in attendance, but was not examined by Mr. Gordon.

CHARGE No. 4.—*Continued.*

WEDNESDAY, March 16th, 1870.

Committee met pursuant to adjournment at 9½ A. M.

Present as before.

R. M. SPRIGG recalled.

By Mr. Schley.

Ques. State whether or not your monthly estimates were not sometimes over and sometimes under what the Division would require?

Ans. Yes.

Ques. What estimate did you make in September for lumber for an ice breaker and house boat for the Seneca Division?

Ans. $800 for the ice breaker and $300 for the house boat.

Ques. Were either of those boats built in September?

Ans. No; they were built in October and November.

Ques. State from your report the entire cost for lumber for those boats?

Ans. $1,664.

Ques. How much of that $1,664 was paid for by the Superintendent of the Seneca Division?

Ans. $800.

Ques. How much was paid for by your Division?

Ans. $864.

Ques. Look and see what the ice breaker for the Seneca Division cost?

Ans. $941.67.

Ques. How much of that was paid for by the Superintendent of the Seneca Division?

Ans. $400.

Ques. How much did that leave to be paid for by you?

Ans. $541.67.

Ques. See what the ice breaker for the Antietam Division cost?

Ans. $941.67.

Ques. How much was paid for by the Superintendent of the Antietam Division?

Ans. $400.

Ques. How much was paid for by you?

Ans. $541.67.

Ques. See what the cost was for the bottom of the house boat for Georgetown Division?
Ans. $706.75.

Ques. How much of that was paid for by the Superintendent of the Georgetown Division?
Ans. $400.

Ques. How much was paid for by you?
Ans. $306.75.

Ques. State to the Committee the whole cost of those four boats?
Ans. $4,254.09.

Ques. How much of that was paid for by the superintendents of the other Divisions?
Ans. $2,000.

Ques. How much did that leave to be paid by you?
Ans. $2,254.09.

Ques. Did you build one ice breaker for yourself, and if so, when?
Ans. I did; in November, 1867, which made the fifth boat I built in that year.

Ques What did that cost?
Ans. $941.67. I paid for that myself.

CUMBERLAND, MD., December 31st, 1868.
To the President and Directors of the Chesapeake and Ohio Canal Company, Washington City, D. C.

Gentlemen:—For the month of December there was little boating on this Division of the canal. Sixty-four boats were loaded between the 1st and the 6th. The canal was closed by ice on the 6th. The ice breaker passed over this Division on the 6th, but the canal would freeze as fast as it was opened. We were obliged to keep them at work night and day to relieve the many boats fast in the ice.

The water has been drawn off at different points on the Division. and some cleaning out has been done at the tunnel for the purpose of repairing and putting in order the trestle work at that point. The tow path, culverts, aqueducts and bridges on this Division are in comparatively good condition. Upon this Division we have twenty locks. extending from Cumberland to dam No. 6, (fifty miles,) thirteen of these are built entirely of wood, (some 19 years since,) except a stone coping at the top. The wear and tear of these locks is very great, not only upon the locks themselves, but upon the gates, on account of their being built of wood. The jarring of boats from side to side will put the gates out of order (or places,) and the pressure of the water will then force them to fly past each other and break off at the post, or the mitre sill will raise up and get out of place. The cause of this is, the wooden locks, which are not and cannot be built as firm and substantial as those built of stone, and they therefore give, to some extent. These locks, as well as the gates, require constant care and repair. We are obliged to keep on hand gates ready made and lumber to repair the gates, as well as locks, and this lumber has to be of assorted sizes, because the lock gates differ in size on account of the difference in the lifts. Some are six armed gates, some seven and some eight, the guard locks ten arm. The locks themselves are of wood, (one hundred feet long,) on each side of the canal filled with stone. The dampness of the ground under and around the locks on account of the leakage of water causes them to sink and give way, and require filling up, and the locks to be adjusted to the size of the gates. From the 1st day of August of this year to the first day of December, we have made and put in seventeen new gates and repaired twenty-three others; we have also put new lining on both sides of seven of the locks, and adjusted and straightened up five others, and have some four or five to new lines this winter. The wear and tear upon these locks and gates this year was greater than in any other previous year, on account of the great or greater number of boats passing through them, some 4,550 boats having passed over this Division of the Canal this year, which is some hundreds more than in any former year; and another cause is on account of the time of the running of the cars over the two railroads that transport coal to the Canal. The time of the loading of the boats is such as to cause them to pass through these locks at night, and make it impossible to use the same care that could be used should they pass through in the day time. From the first of last fall to the end of the boating season the coal companies shipping by the Canal put all their boats running at night and day. The amount of lumber bought for the use of this Division, from the first of August to the first of December, was the amount of $4,146.11. This was used in the repairs of locks and gates, building new gates, repairing road bridges at Wiley's Ford, one new ice ice breaker for the use of this Division, repairing lock house at Old Town, putting in one new waste weir at Sidling Hill Creek, and building a blacksmith shop at the tunnel.

We have on hand the sides and timber for a mud machine,
   worth about...$300 00
Lumber for extension or use of the Canal basin................ 206 62
Also, for one waste weir, to be put in at Old Town............ 100 00
And new lock gate timber... 200 00

                                                                                      $806 62

Dressed flooring was purchased for sealing the house boat and the building of the cabin for the ice breaker built here for the use of the Seneca Division, and the cabin of the ice breaker built for the use of the Antietam Division, and the deck of the scow built for the use of house boat on the Georgetown Division, amounting to $346.00 paid for by this Division; and two derricks built for the Hancock Division, to be used in repairing the culverts on that Division, amounting to $225.00.

The cost of the house boat built for the Seneca Division was,

Lumber	$879 25
Iron, nails, spikes and bolts	85 25
Oakum, pitch and caulking	33 00
Painting and glazing	81 00
Workmanship, &c	555 50
	$1,664 00
Paid by the Superintendent of the Seneca Division for lumber	800 00
	$864 00

The cost of the ice breaker built for the use of the Seneca Division,

Lumber	$491 00
Iron, spikes, nails and bolts	168 17
Oakum, pitch and caulking	63 00
Painting and glazing	18 00
Workmanship	201 50
	$941 67
Paid by the Superintendent of the Seneca Division for lumber	400 00
	$541 67

Cost of the ice breaker built for the use of the Antietam Division,

Lumber	$491 00
Iron, spikes, nails and bolts	168 17
Oakum, pitch and caulking	63 00
Painting and glazing	18 00
Workmanship	201 50
	$941 67
Amount paid by Superintendent of Antietam Division for lumber	400 00
Balance	$541 67

Cost of the scow built for the house boat for the Georgetown Division,

Lumber	$400 00
Iron, spikes, nails and bolts	34 75
Oakum, pitch and caulking	63 00
Workmanship	209 00
	$706 75
Paid by Superintendent of Georgetown Division	400 00
	$306 75

The whole cost of these boats being	$4,254 09
And the amounts paid by Superintendents of different Divisions being	2,000 00
	$2,254 09
Amounts for derricks for use of Hancock Division	225 00
Balance	$2,479 09

The construction of these ice breakers is as follows: Four pine sides, 60 feet long, 12 inches wide and 6 inches thick; two of these sides are put together on each side on the edge, and are bolted together by iron bolts of 1½ inch round iron and 28 inches long, one oak piece 3 inches thick and 6 inches wide, put on the outside and bolted together by bolts of 1 inch round iron 24 inches long, making (at the bottom) 15 inches of solid timber extending entire length of the boat (on each side.) The bow has a rake extending back 13 feet, made of oak timber, ironed with $\frac{3}{8}$ inch sheet iron the entire width of the boat at the bottom, and extending up 2 feet on each side; around the bow and stern they are ironed with bar iron 3x½ flat iron; the post of 2 inch round iron, the steering blade of ¼ inch sheet iron, the inside timbers are all 6 inches square. These boats will break ice from one to six inches thick with ease, having double the strength of the usual scow, they are also useful and good repair boats on the line of the canal, the deck being composed of 2 inch timber. In my return for the month of September of this year, I estimated the building of two of these boats at $800 each, one to the Seneca Division and one to the Antietam Division, and lumber for the house boat for the Seneca Division at $300. This was an error, which I beg leave to correct, as I understood at first the order for the building of these boats to be that I was to use the lumber then on hand for the building of lock gates and repairs of lock bridges, and the lumber on hand for the building of ice breaker for the use of this Division. In this I was mistaken, and therefore caused the error in the estimate, and my putting it in the returns of that month No part of these boats was built in August or September, nor was any part of the lumber purchased in August, September, October or November used in the construction of them except as heretofore stated. The sum of $346 was paid for dressed flooring for sheeting the house boat, doors, &c., cabins for the two ice breakers and the deck of the scow for the use of the house boat on the Georgetown Division. The trestle work at the tunnel will be repaired as by direction of the Board, the locks and lock gates repaired and put in good order, the basin at Cumberland cleaned out, the rotten and sunken boats taken out, the waste weirs examined and repaired, one new one put in at Old Town, the canal well cleaned out, and the entire Division put in good boating order for the coming season.

All of which is respectfully submitted for your consideration.

Very respectfully, &c.,

Your obedient servant,

(Signed,) R. M. SPRIGG.

OFFICE OF THE CHESAPEAKE & OHIO CANAL CO.

WASHINGTON CITY, November 16, 1868.

RICH'D M. SPRIGG, ESQ.,
Sup't Cumberland Division, Cumberland, Md.

Dear Sir :—Your accounts for the month of October have been received and examined.

Months' expenses for services		$2,324 52
For bills	$2,191 53	
Less for error in addition of J. K. Brown & Co's. bill, (No. 68.)	$33 54	
Should be	23 54	
	$ 10 00	
		$2,181 53
Total expenses, and cash paid out for the month		$4,506 05
Cash due Superintendent at the first of the month		1,152 07
		$5,658 12
Cash received for the month—check for		4,500 00
Cash due R. M. Sprigg, Sup't, at the close of the month		$1,158 12

Yours truly,

BENJ. FAWCETT,

Clerk.

Ques. Did you receive any letter from the office showing an over payment upon your part?

Ans. I did, and this is it. (Marked letter of B. Fawcett, November 16th, 1868, showing cash due R. M. Sprigg at the close of the month, $1,158.12.)

Ques. Your estimate was for $1,900. State now exactly what you paid out on those four boats?
Ans. $2,254.09.

Ques. Did you not ouild two derricks for the Hancock Division?
Ans. I did.

Ques. State what they cost?
Ans. $225.

Ques. That makes your actual expenses for that month—how much on other Divisions?
Ans. $2,479.09.

Ques. Do you know how many feet of lumber generally come on one car?
Ans. From 10,000 to 12,000 feet.

Ques. In getting a car from a distance, do they not charge as much for a half load as for a whole one?
Ans. They do.

Ques. What was that sort of lumber generally worth?
Ans. $40 per M.

Cross-Examination by Mr. Gordon.

Ques. Look at your abstract for September, 1868, and state how much money the Canal Company paid you on it?
Ans. $6,600, which, with $42.42 I had on hand, makes $6,642.42.

Ques. That left a balance in your favor of how much?
Ans. $1,152.07.

Ques. Did you get that afterwards?
Ans. I did.

Ques. Look at that abstract and state if it has been altered, and if so, when the alteration was made?
Ans. It was altered before it went in to the Board. Mr. Lowe, who made it out, had put in work I had not done, and work that I had done he omitted. I did not want to deface it, and pasted that paper over it.

Ques. Why did you make separate charges of part of the cost of building these boats to the other Divisions?
Ans. I was ordered by the Board to charge the expenses of the boats that went to other Divisions in the way they are entered on the abstract. It gave me a great deal of trouble to keep the accounts separate. I rely entirely upon my report for my information about these matters.

Ques. What do you mean by saying your estimates are sometimes above and sometimes below what you require?

Ans. The estimates showed how much money would probably be required. The abstracts showed how much had actually been expended.

Ques. Look at your abstract for October, 1868, and state how much money you received on that?

Ans. $4,500.

Ques. Look at your abstract for December, 1868, and state how much money you received on it?

Ans. $4,500.

Ques. Look at your abstract for November, 1868, and state how much money you received on that?

Ans. $6,200.

Ques. Did that pay you the balance left over from September?

Ans. It did, and left a balance in my hands of $131.90.

Ques. In what months was all this lumber bought, you mention on your report?

Ans. August, September, October and November.

Ques. Is it all covered by your monthly reports for those months?

Ans. All that we used is covered by them, but a great deal of it was distributed along the Canal to make repairs during the winter.

Ques. How much lumber does it take to make one lock gate?

Ans. In the neighborhood of 2,000 feet.

Ques. What sort of material do you use for lining locks?

Ans. Two inch and one and a half inch, or one and a quarter inch lumber.

Ques. Describe to the Committee how they are made.

Ans. It is a frame-work of 8x10 inch stuff, two feet apart, up and down the whole length, that is covered with two inch lumber, and then covered with one and a half or one and a quarter inch, up and down, next to the locks.

Ques. How long were the locks?

Ans. One hundred feet.

Ques. What height?

Ans. Some sixteen feet, some eighteen feet.

Ques. What does the two inch lumber cost?

Ans. From $2.50 to $3 a hundred.

Ques. How much lumber does it take to build a derrick?

Ans. I do not know.

Ques. How many lock gates did you repair, and what amount of repairs?

Ans. Twenty-three. Some required a good deal and some not much repair. Put new fenders on all and on some new balance-beams. The beams were twenty-four feet long, and sixteen by eighteen inches, and there was from four hundred to five hundred feet in each beam. The amount of lumber used at each gate would average from five hundred to six hundred feet.

By Mr. Schley.

Ques. Is your report verified by your monthly abstracts?
Ans. It is.

Ques. Was there not a good deal of complaint by the Board of Directors about keeping your accounts separate, and did they not want you to show what was spent on your Division and what for other Divisions?

Ans. Yes, sir.

Ques. Look at the summary on your abstract for September, 1868, and see if you find an amount for repairing a break, and if so, read out the amount.

Ans. I do. For repairing break near twenty-seven mile post, $3,514.50.

Ques. Look at the paper, (marked rough estimate, referred to by Mr. Sprigg in his testimony,) and state whether it is an estimate made by you for lumber used during August, September, October and November, 1868, and read it.

Ans. It is.

"Seventeen new lock gates, lumber............................$1,700 00
Twenty-three gates repaired, lumber........................... 575 00
Seven locks, lining on the side................................. 350 00
Five locks repaired... 50 00
Lumber for extension of basin................................. 206 62
Waste weir at Old Town.. 100 00
Lock gate timber on hand....................................... 200 00
Seneca, Antietam and Georgetown flooring, decking and
  lining, sealing, &c.. 352 25
Two derricks to Hancock, lumber............................. 100 00
Lumber for Sprigg's ice breaker.............................. 491 00
                                                            —————
                                                            $4,124 87

Ques. Is that paper correct?
Ans. It may be over, it may be under the amount actually used.

By Mr. Gordon.

Ques. By what process did you arrive at those different items.
Ans. I merely guessed at them.

Ques. How many feet of one and a quarter inch lumber does it require to line one side of a lock seventeen feet high and ninety feet long?

Ans. From eighteen to nineteen hundred feet.

Ques. How many feet in one of those balance beams?

Ans. They vary from three hundred and fifty to six hundred feet.

Ques. You say you are not certain this estimate is correct; how much might it be over or under?

Ans. I do not know.

Ques. Is your report correct?

Ans. Yes, sir.

Ques. How much does it differ from your report?

Ans. About $21 less.

By Mr. Schley.

Ques. How long is your Division?

Ans. 50 miles. It extends to Dam No. 6.

Ques. How did you proceed to make your report?

Ans. I went to the lower end of my Division, and made a note of all repairs as I went along throughout the whole line.

Ques. How many locks are on your Division?

Ans. Twenty; thirteen wooden, and the balance stone.

Ques. Do, or do not, those wooden locks require constant repairs?

Ans. They do.

Ques. Did you leave the locks all in good repair?

Ans. I did; and also left about 30,000 feet of lumber on hand, all paid for.

R. M. SPRIGG.

CLEMENT A. PECK recalled.

By Mr. Gordon.

Ques. Were you in the service of the Canal Company in 1867?

Ans. Yes, sir.

Ques. When did Mr. Fawcett become connected with the Canal?

Ans. On 1st May, 1868, I think.

Ques. Who was the Superintendent of the Monocacy Division in 1867?

Ans. George W. Spates, I think.

Ques. When was the new Division made?

Ans. I do not know.

Ques. Out of what portion of the line was that Division made?

Ans. Part of the Georgetown and part of the Monocacy.

Ques. Who was Superintendent of the new Division?

Ans. George W. Spates.

Ques. Look at those vouchers of Mr. Spates, (G. W.,) and state whether you have any knowledge of their being filed in the office in 1867?

Ans. There is nothing by which I could tell that these are the vouchers—that looks like my hand-writing on the wrapper.

Mr. Schley objected to this examination, as he had asked witness nothing in chief in regard to this matter.

Mr. Gordon said his object was to show that G. W. Spates returned his vouchers marked in that way from 1867 down, and wished to compare the mark on these vouchers with the mark on the Tasker vouchers.

Ques. I understood you to say yesterday evening that whenever a Superintendent failed to return a voucher with his abstract, you made a note of it and wrote to him?

Ans. Yes, sir.

Ques. There is nothing to indicate that Spates neglected to return vouchers for the Tasker bills?

Ans. No, sir.

Ques. Look at George W. Spates' vouchers for November, 1868, and see if they are not numbered in the same manner.

Ans. They seem to be all marked in the same way.

Ques. Are they marked on the abstract in the same way.

Ans. Yes, the numbers correspond with the numbers on the voucher.

Ques. Was it not your business to compare the vouchers with the abstract?

Ans. I compared the amounts but never took particular notice of the numbers. I generally observed that they were numbered, but noticed sometimes that the numbers did not exactly correspond, but supposed the mistake occurred in making a copy of the abtract.

By Mr. Schley.

Ques. Whilst in the office did you ever have any abstracts returned to you in which the distribution of the summary was not made out?

Ans. Frequently. I think it will be found that the distribution on Mr. Maus statements is nearly all in my handwriting. I never looked upon that as a matter of much importance. For the last few months I was there, there was no means of telling what the money was expended for, except to look at the payments for labor and the bills.

By Mr. Schley.

Ques. Look at the " Proceedings of President and Directors," p. 167, and state if there is a paper pasted on that page.
Ans. There is.

Ques. Do you know why that was done?
Ans. I do not.

CLEMENT A. PECK.

A. K. STAKE sworn.

By Mr. Schley.

Ques. Were you a Director in the Canal in 1868?
Ans. Yes.

Ques. Do you, or not, recollect that a report was ordered to be made by Mr. Sprigg, Superintendent of the Cumberland Division, and if so, was that report made?
Ans. He was directed to make a report and he made one.

Ques. To whom was it referred?
Ans. To the Committee on Accounts.

Ques. Did you, or not, have occasion to use that report for any purpose?
Ans. We had it before the Board and gave it a cursory examination, after which it was referred to the Committee on Accounts. My recollection about it is that it did not seem to be satisfactory upon its face until compared with the regular abstracts. I read the report to the Board and took the pains to compare it with the abstracts and to verify it by them, and this examination seemed to be satisfactory to the Board.

Ques. Do you not recollect at the time you had that report whether or not there were any copies of bills for expenses for other Divisions?
Ans. There were copies of bills for material furnished other Divisions.

Ques. Have you any recollection what bills they were?
Ans. I cannot say certainly. Some of them were lumber bills.

Ques. Did not Col. Spates, President of the Canal Company, ask and urge you to vote for Mr. Fawcett as Clerk?
Ans. Yes, sir.

Ques. Did you, or not, do it?
Ans. No, sir. I was not present at the meeting. I however said I would not vote to turn Mr. Ringgold out.

Cross-Examination by Mr. Gordon.

Ques. Why was that report required?

Ans. The expenses of the Cumberland Division, growing out of the building of those boats, appeared to be out of proportion with the expenses of the other Divisions, and the inquiry was raised in the Board on several occasions as to the cause of this, and from that the Board requested Mr. Sprigg to make this report, which order was passed at a meeting in the latter part of 1868.

Ques. Was it not an extraordinary thing to require a report of this kind?

Ans. It was not. The Superintendents were frequently called on to make explanations of their reports.

---

4 o'clock, P. M.

GEORGE HUGHES recalled.

By Mr. Schley.

Ques. Do you know Ezekiel Male, of Cumberland?

Ans. I do.

Ques. State whether or not you had a conversation with Male in in reference to lumber furnished to the Canal Company by Tasker & Co.?

Ans. I had, on last Sunday three weeks ago. He told me he had to unload $3\frac{1}{2}$ car loads of lumber for the Canal Company; that the greater part of the half car was for the Canal Company. The cars contained from 10,000 to 11,000 feet of lumber each. He said the lumber came from Tasker & Co's., and that he had likewise hauled from the yard from 1500 to 1800 feet for the Canal Company.

Ques. Do you know the price of that lumber?

Ans. The greater portion or it is worth $4.00 per hundred.

By Mr. Gordon.

Ques. Did you say that you had 25 mules attached to that ice breaker at one time?

Ans. I had for a short time, probably one or two hours.

GEORGE HUGHES.

C. SLACK sworn.

By Mr. Schley.

Ques. Was H. P. Tasker a partner of yours in Cumberland?

Ans. He was from July 1868 to about the 1st of Feb. 1869.

Ques. When you dissolved partnership what share did Tasker get of the stock of goods?

Ans. I do not know that he received any distributive share of the profits of the concern. The business had not gone on satisfactorily to the parties who furnished the building and capital, and we made arrangements with him to go out of the concern, and gave him $500 for doing so.

Ques. What was your stock of goods worth at that time?

Ans. About $12,000 or $15,000.

Ques. At the time of the dissolution did you take stock, so as to see what was his distributive share?

Ans. We did not. Our arrangement with him was, we were to pay him a salary of $900 for his active management of the business.

Ques. Who furnished the lumber of your business?

Ans. It came from various places; most of it from David Tasker's mill?

Ques. State to the Committee whether there was any difficulty about the lumber account?

Ans. There was. At the time of the dissolution there was a very considerable deficiency in the lumber account.

By Mr. Gordon.

Ques. How do you know that?

Ans. The lumber was measured and sold and returns made. I saw the papers myself. When the measurement came in it was compared with the lumber account.

Ques. Did you settle in accordance with that measurement?

Ans. We did not, but decided to have a re-measurement, to which Mr. Tasker was a party. I never saw the last measurement.

Ques. Did you ever have a conversation with Mr. Tasker about it?

Ans. I did. I urged him to become a party to the re-measurement for his own credit's sake.

Ques. What was the amount of that deficiency?

Ans. 30,000 or 40,000 feet. The books will show that fact.

By Mr. Gordon.

Ques. Are not the books the best evidence?

Ans. I should think so.

Ques. How much lumber passed through your hands in a year?

Ans. Something like half a million of feet.

Ques. Do you know whether they received the lumber by the measurement of the mill?

Ans. I do not.

C. SLACK.

AMOS THOMAS sworn.

By Mr. Poe.

Ques. Were you Superintendent of the Monocacy Division of the Chesapeake and Ohio Canal Company in April and May, 1869?

Ans. Yes, sir.

Ques. Did you apply to your Company for a scow and mud machine for your Division in the Spring of 1869?

Ans. Yes, sir.

Ques. Please to state whether Mr. Spates, President of the Company, undertook to have the scow furnished from Cumberland, and whether you drew from the Canal Company the money to pay for it?

Ans. Mr. Spates undertook to furnish the scow. The money never passed through my hands. My father brought me the voucher for the $350 paid for the scow.

Ques. Did he get the voucher from Mr. Spates?

Ans. I do not know.

Ques. Did you return that voucher to the office of the Canal Company with your abstract?

Ans. I did.

Ques. Look at the paper now shown to you, (marked receipt of Henry Snyder for $350,) and see whether that is the voucher?

Ans. That looks like my No. 49. If that is the voucher I sent to the office it is the one he gave me.

Ques. Is this your monthly abstract (marked abstract of Amos Thomas for April, 1869?)

Ans. Yes, sir.

Ques. Are the words, Henry Snyder, $350, in your hand-writing, on the list of bills paid?

Ans. They are.

Ques. Did you charge the bill and receipt of Henry Snyder amongst your expenditures for that month?

Ans. Yes, sir.

Ques. Did you file the receipt as a voucher?

Ans. I did.

Cross-Examination by Mr. Schley.

Ques. Did you get the scow and mud machine?
Ans. Yes, sir.

Ques. How long did you have it before it was paid for?
Ans. I had it some time; I don't remember how long.

Ques. Look at that paper (marked letter of Amos Thomas, March 30, 1869,) and see if it is your letter?

Ans. It is.

Ques. Please read it?

Ans. "March 30th, 1869. To the President and Directors of Chesapeake and Ohio Canal: The Monocacy Division, under my charge, is in complete and good navigable condition. I let the water on the entire Division 12th inst. I am progressing slowly. I will, as soon as the water in the Potomac river will permit, I shall finish the riprapping at that point along the canal at Weverton, which, I think, ought to be done as soon as possible. Scow and mud machine is very badly wanting.

Most respectfully,

(Signed) AMOS THOMAS,
Sup't."

Ques. Look at that paper (marked letter of Amos Thomas, May 3d, 1869,) and see if it is your letter?

Ans. Yes, sir.

Ques. Please read it?

Ans. "May 3rd, 1869. To the President and Directors of Chesapeake and Ohio Canal Company: I respectfully report that the Monocacy Division, under my charge, has been in a good, navigable condition up to date. The heavy rains and high waters early in April caused a portion of the northern side of the culvert east of the Point of Rocks to give way, but by timely notice prevented any interruption of navigation. I have no scow on that part of the Division until to-day. I get an old one sent me by the President, and now, as soon as possible, I will get the kind of stone to repair the culvert, so no further trouble may be expected from it. I am also laboring under great disadvantage for the want of a mud machine to keep clear the mud from the mouth of the feeder at dam No. 3. * * *

(Signed) AMOS THOMAS,
Sup't."

Ques. Was the scow worth $350?

Ans. It was. I thought it cheap at that. It was not a new scow.

AMOS THOMAS.

CHARGE No. 5.

A. K. STAKE recalled.

By Mr. Schley.

Ques. Look at the book of proceedings of the Board, March 3d, 1869, page 149, and state whether there was not an order passed to get certain boats, &c.?

Ans. The following resolution was passed at a meeting at which I was present: "On motion, it was ordered that the President and General Superintendent have constructed and built for the use of Monocacy, Antietam, and other Divisions of the Canal, one mud machine; also, one scow for the use of the Monocacy Division, said mud machine and scow to be paid for by the Superintendent of the Monocacy Division upon the presentation of the bills of cost for the same by the President and General Superintendent."

Ques. State whether about that time or afterwards you knew anything about a scow belonging to a man named Snyder, being purchased for the Canal?

Ans. Shortly after the passage of the order, the President, Mr. Spates, consulted me in regard to some scows that had been used in the construction of the Government dam at Harper's Ferry, and asked me if I knew anything about them. I told him they were not in use any more, and if there were any scows there they would probably be useful ones. He told me that there was one there that had been offered to him for sale by a man named Snyder, and that the man asked $400 for it. I told him that a scow lying there so short a time and still afloat, would be worth that money. I heard nothing more about it until I met Col. Spates at Weverton, to examine into some difficulty about the lock, upon which occasion he told me he had bought the scow from the party named, and that he had got it for $300.

Cross-Examination by Mr. Gordon.

Ques. At what time was the Government dam built?
Ans. About 1860 or 1861.

Ques. Do you know where those scows had been all that time?
Ans. I do not.

Ques. Do you know anything about their condition?
Ans. Nothing further than what I stated to Col Spates, that if they had been used but a short time, and were still floating, they would be useful scows.

JAMES J. McHENRY sworn.

By Mr. Poe.

Ques. State where you live?
Ans. In Cumberland, Allegany county.

Ques. What is your profession?
Ans. I am a lawyer.

Ques. Look at that paper, (marked receipt of Henry Snyder, $350,) and state to the Committee in whose handwriting it is?

Ans. It is in my handwriting, with the exception of the signature.

Ques. State at whose instance you prepared that paper and the circumstances?

Ans. About a year and a half ago I was coming down Baltimore street, in Cumberland, in the afternoon, after the cars came in from Baltimore, and when I came to the corner of Baltimore and Centre streets, I saw Mr. Spates standing on the corner, and some one was with him. As I came up, Mr. Spates said, "Mack, I wish you would come in and make out a little bill for me. I want to pay this man, who wants to get his money to go home this evening." I don't pretend to give his language, but that is the impression what he said created on my mind. I went into the store of J. and T. Coulehan, and made out one bill, and Mr. Spates observed, "Make out another one. I have to keep duplicates." I did so, and afterwards he and I walked out the front door together, and the person who was with him went away with him.

Ques. Did he dictate the terms of the bill to you?

Ans. Yes, sir.

Ques. Did you know that Amos Thomas was Superintendent of the Monocacy Division at that time?

Ans. I did not. The whole of that information was derived from Mr. Spates.

Ques. Was the paper signed when it passed out of your hands?

Ans. It was not.

Ques. Was there any stamp on it?

Ans. There was not.

Ques. You are on terms of familiar intimacy with Mr. Spates, are you not?

Ans. I am. I have for the last eighteen years been in the habit of writing letters for Mr. Spates, and often making copies and fixing up papers time and again, so that asking this little favor was not an unusual thing.

Cross-Examination by Mr. Schley.

Ques. You have seen Henry Snyder here?

Ans. Yes, sir.

Ques. Was that the man with Mr. Spates?

Ans. It was not. The man with Mr. Spates was a stranger to me.

By Mr. Poe.

Ques. Do you know of any other Henry Snyder, a boat builder, in Cumberland?

Ans. I do not.

Ques. How long have you lived in Cumberland?

Ans. Twenty-four years.

By Mr. Schley.

Ques. Do you recollect, or not, whether Mr. Spates told you where the man lived that was with him at that time?

Ans. There is an impression on my mind that he either said Hancock or Seneca Division.

Mr. Poe.

Ques. You say you have lived in Cumberland twenty-four years; do you know Thomas Sheridan?

Ans. Very well.

Ques. Do you know any Thomas Sheridan engaged in boat building, except Thomas Sheridan, the foreman of Mr. Weld?

Ans. I do not. He has a son of that name, a youth.

Ques. Might there be a man doing a job of work at that kind and you know nothing about it?

Ans. There might be, but there is no other Thomas Sheridan known to the community but Thomas Sheridan, the agent of Henry Thomas Weld.

By Mr. Schley.

Ques. Might there not have been a Thomas Sheridan building a boat in the yard of the Chesapeake and Ohio Canal Company and you not know it?

Ans. There might have been. There are a great many men there I do not know at all.

Ques. Did you ever know of two scows being built on the ground where the first wharf was, on the left hand side going from my office, when two men came there and built those scows, and afterwards disappeared?

Ans. I do recollect something of the kind, but do not know who they were.

By Mr. Poe.

Ques. Look at that bill of Thomas Sheridan's and see if you know the handwriting?

Ans. I cannot say whose handwriting it is.

Mr. Gordon.

Ques. State whether the paper (marked True Copy of Record of Inquisition proved by Mr. McHenry) is in your handwriting?

Ans. It is all in my handwriting except the signature of the clerk.

Ques. Is that a correct copy?

Ans. It is. I made it out from the original papers.

J. J. McHENRY.

CHARGE No. 6.

Mr. Schley offered in evidence the following letter:

CUMBERLAND, September 14th, 1869.

MR. ALFRED SPATES,

Sir:—It appears by the books and proceedings of the Chesapeake and Ohio Canal Company that the sum of $10,000 was placed by that Company in your hands while you were its President, for the purpose of paying for condemnations of land at Cumberland, and it also appears that in settling with the Canal Company for that sum of $10,000, you claimed and received credit for the sum of $739 paid by J. Philip Roman, for the Canal Company, to Josiah H Gordon, as attorney for Henry Thomas Weld and wife, for condemnation in No. 163, trials to April term, 1868, in the Circuit Court for Allegany county, being for $725 damages and the cost in the case of Weld and wife for the right of way for the towing bridge of the Rose Hill Wharf Company across the mouth of Wills creek.

It also appears by a receipt of J. Philip Roman, as attorney of the Canal Company, to the Rose Hill Wharf Company, that Mr. Roman received said sum of money from the Wharf Company, and that it has therefore been paid by the Canal Company and the Wharf Company both, or else you have claimed and received a credit for that amount of money from the Canal Company, which you did not pay, and have no right to. I would be glad to have your explanation of this matter at once, as I am required to make a report to the committee of accounts of the Canal Company, which is now waiting my reply.

Yours, &c.,

(Signed)   J. H. GORDON,
Pres't Ches. and Ohio Canal Co.

JOSIAH H. GORDON sworn.

By Mr. Schley.

Ques. At the time you wrote that letter to Col. Spates were you and he on speaking terms?

Ans. No, sir.

Ques. Be kind enough to state to the Committee, after you wrote that letter and it got into the possession of Col. Spates, the interview that took place between you, and where it took place?

Ans. The first interview between him and me, after that letter was written, took place at the railroad. Just as I was going to dinner, about two o'clock in the afternoon, I was passing by the railroad, and Mr. Spates, who was standing there, mentioned to me that he had received my note. We had some conversation there, but I do not remember exactly what it was. He said he had the money in bank, and would place it to the credit of the Canal Company, and said something about an explanation, and I told him he had better make it in writing. He said that would not be necessary, as he would place the money to the credit of the Canal Company.

By Mr. Spates.

Ques. When I approached you, did I, or not, say to you that I knew nothing in the world about this thing?

Ans. I think you did.

Ques. Did I, or not, say, Mr. Gordon, if that record is dated 1868 it is a mistake, that it did not take place in my administration, but in that of Snivley's?

Ans. I do not remember anything of the kind.

Ques. Are you certain I did not say that?

Ans. I do not say you did not. I say I do not remember.

MARCH 23d.

Mr. Gordon being recalled at his own request, says that he has refreshed his memory in regard to the matter of the date of the record, and now says that he does recollect that Mr. Spates said to him in the conversation at the depot that if the record is dated in 1868, it is a mistake, it did not take place in my administration, but in that of Snivley.

Ques. Did I not say to you that I had nothing to do with this thing, but would go to the bank and investigate it and come to your office and show to you the whole transaction—that it had all been done by Roman?

Ans. Yes, sir; you told me that.

Ques. Did I not come to your office about four o'clock on that same day, and did I not there exhibit to you there all the checks in this case?

Ans. You came to my office, but I do not know whether you exhibited all the checks in this case. You exhibited some checks, I do not know how many. I looked over some of them, and saw they were in Mr. Roman's hand-writing.

Ques. Did I not say to you there that this money was never paid out by me; it was all paid out by Mr. Roman, and I do find he never paid this amount, and I have had it transferred to the credit of the Company?

Ans. I do not remember that you said Mr. Roman never paid this amount, but you said he had charge of the whole thing, and had drawn the checks upon the fund. That you said.

Ques. Did I not say that this was a mistake, that I knew nothing about it, and had transferred the amount to the Company?

Ans. Yes, sir; that you said.

Ques. Did I not make this remark after you had looked over the checks, "Mr. Gordon there is no offence in your note. I have approached you because of the latter part of it: that seemed friendly to me, it had a friendly tone, for you and I had never had any difference?"

Ans. Yes, sir.

Ques. Upon presenting to you these checks, you took them and looked them over. Did you or not, then make this remark: "Yes, I see how the business was done, and how very readily a mistake of that kind might occur?"

Ans. I do not remember that, but I recollect distinctly of your showing me the receipts—I do not know how many—I think they were all in Mr. Roman's hand-writing.

Ques. Did not I show a disposition to show you everything in regard to it, and to make any and every explanation?

Ans. I have said exactly the explanation you did make.

Qes. Did you not receive it as satisfactory at the time?

Ans. Not in regard to the $739, because you had no receipt for that.

Ques. Then it was understood between you and me that it was settled?

Ans. Yes, sir; that settled that amount of it.

Ques. Then, Mr. Gordon, why was it a week after you published your circular?

Ans. For the reason that you had been making statements in regard to me, Mr. Spates. Then I will be sworn that you were misinformed, and be your author whom he may I will face him.

Ques. Were these the checks I exhibited to you, or any part of them. (Marked J. P. Roman's check to T. J. McKaig, August 1, 1868, $6400; J. P. Roman's check to T. J. McKaig, April 7, 1868, $1000; J. P. Roman's check to T. J. McKaig, August 18, 1868, $1000; J. P. Roman's check to Jacob Earlougher, March 28, 1868, $850; J. P. Roman's check to D. Duncan, September 5, 1868, $55.60?)

Ans. These four for $6400, $1000, $1000 and $850, I recollect distinctly: that for $55.60, I do not remember.

Mr. Schley offered in evidence the certificate of Edwin A. Moore, addressed to Benj. Fawcett, Treasurer of the Chesapeake and Ohio Canal Company stating that Col. A. Spates had placed to the credit of the Canal Company $739.

J. M. SCHLEY sworn.

I desire to make an explanation in regard to the check for $55.60. After the condemnation was made by the Canal Company of the property of Henry Thomas Weld and wife for a tow-path, it was discovered that the abutment of the tow-path bridge upon the west side of Wills creek seemed to stand upon the property of the Cumberland Coal and Iron Company. The Mount Savage Iron Company was to pay one-third of the cost of that bridge, but after they discovered that it stood upon property claimed by the Cumberland Coal and Iron Company they refused to pay their proportion until it was condemned. I instructed J. Philip Roman, as counsel for the Canal Company, to take out a writ of inquisition, which he did, and had the property condemned, but, to his utter astonishment, it was afterwards found that no notice had ever been served upon the Cumberland Coal and Iron Company. Of course the condemnation was null and void; the $55.60 was the Sheriff's fees, which was paid by Mr. Roman, and which ought never to have been paid by the Canal Company.

CHARGE No. 8.

R. M. SPRIGG recalled.

By Mr. Schley.

Ques. Look at your abstract for April, 1868, and see if you find on it any charge to Lewis Miller, and, if so, state the amount?

Ans. I paid him $1,452.

Ques. Look at the receipt of A. L. Miller for $1,452, and state whether that is the one you filed with your abstract?

Ans. It is; I have the duplicate.

Ques. For what did you pay that amount?

Ans. "For tearing up and removing forty boats in Cumberland basin, at $36.30 per boat."

Ques. Was that all the money the Canal Company paid for that purpose?

Ans. Yes, sir.

Ques. Was there any money paid by anybody else for that purpose?

Ans. There were some other boats to be moved, and I got men to do it, for which they charged $104. Mr. Spates gave me $100, and I settled with them for that amount.

Ques. Do you or not know of any arrangement with A. Willison for shutting off the water from his mill?

Ans. The boats could not be removed without shutting off the water from Mr. Willison's mill. He wanted $50 per day for shutting it off. I agreed to give him $40 per day for eleven days. The Canal Company did not pay this money. Mr. Spates paid it.

Ques. How came you to have these boats taken out?

Ans. The Court indicted the Canal Company and the corporation, for allowing these boats to lie in the basin. Mr. Humbird told me I must have them taken out, but I would not take the responsibility without an order from Mr. Spates. I telegraphed to him, but could not find him anywhere. Mr. Roman told me to take them out, and Mr. Humbird said he would stand between me and harm if I did it. I went on and the work to the amount of $1,452. and had the boats all out before Mr. Spates came back. He was worried a good deal about it, and threatened to turn me off for it, and said the Canal Company should not pay any more than had been paid.

Ques. Do you know anything about how the corporation raised the money to pay Mr. Willison $540.

Ans. They gave Mr. Spates a draft at four months for that amount and he paid the money.

Cross-Examination by Mr. Gordon.

Ques. When did you get the duplicate receipt from Miller?

Ans. At the same time I got the other. I never pay anybody without taking duplicate receipts.

JOHN HUMBIRD sworn.

By Mr. Schley.

Ques. Were you Mayor of Cumberland at the time these boats were removed from the Canal basin, in March, 1868?

Ans. I was.

Ques. State whether or not you had any conversation with Richard Sprigg with reference to the removal of those boats, and if so, state that conversation?

Ans. When Mr. Sprigg got through with taking the first boats from the Canal basin he notified me that the Canal Company had done all the work they intended to do. I had notified Mr. Spates in the meantime at Annapolis, by letter, that they should go on and clean out the basin, believing at the time it belonged to the Canal Company. He paid no attention to my letters, and I called on Mr. Sprigg and he told me he had no authority to clean out the basin. I then told him to go ahead and clean it out and he should be paid; if the Canal Company did not pay it the city would pay it.

Ques. Did, or did not, the corporation make any arrangement to pay Mr. Willison for shutting the water off his mill?

Ans. There was a draft given to Col. Spates for $540, from the corporation. The understanding was this. We were scarce of money at the time and I refused to pay the claim and the Canal Company refused to pay it. Finally, Mr. Sprigg complained to me that I had put him to work, and had promised him that there should be no difficulty between him and the Canal Company. I then agreed if Colonel Spates would furnish the money to issue this draft with the understanding that Col. Spates was to take the draft and pay the claims. The draft was issued and handed over to Col. Spates.

Ques. Was that, or not, the debt of the City Council for which they issued their draft to Col. Spates?

Ans. The city agreed to pay the $540 and issued the draft with the understanding that he was to pay those claims.

JOHN HUMBIRD.

ASAHEL WILLISON sworn.

By Mr. Schley.

Ques. Where do you live?
Ans. In Cumberland.

Ques. What is your occupation?
Ans. I have a mill.

Ques. Had you a mill in March, 1868?
Ans. I had.

Ques. State whether or not you had any arrangement with the Canal Company, or with any other party, in regard to shutting off the water from your mill at the time those boats were cleaned out of the basin?

Ans. I had an arrangement with the Canal Company to shut the water off my mill for a few days for $40 per day. It had been shut off three or four days when Mr. Sprigg, the Superintendent, told me he did not want the water shut off any longer, and that I could turn it on. Mr. Humbird, the Mayor, came with him, or directly afterwards, and asked me not to put the water on, that there were other boats to be cleaned out by some person. He thought the Canal Company was the proper party to do it, and asked me still to continue to keep the water off; that he, as Mayor, would see that I was paid for it. About the same time the agents of the Cumberland Coal and Iron Company insisted on my keeping it off. Mr. Sprigg would not agree that he would pay for the work until Mr. Humbird told him that he would be protected in doing it, and to accommodate them, as it was the season for cleaning out nuisances, that he must take his hands and assist in cleaning the other basin. So, of course, I knew I was in safe hands. I still continued to keep the water off for eleven days, at the rate of $40 per day. Mr. Spates came home a few days after the work had been done, and, coming to see me about it, asked me something about stopping my mill. I told him Mr. Sprigg had bargained with me. He was very much enraged about Mr. Sprigg's conduct as he thought; and I then told Mr. Spates that Mr. Sprigg was not to blame, and told him then what I tell now. He said he should never pay a dollar of this expenditure, so the matter rested there. I did not get any money for my work for two months afterwards, when I tried to collect it of the Cumberland Coal and Iron Company. The corporation said the Canal Company should pay it. I called on Mr. Spates, and he told me the Canal Company had no right to pay for any but the first few days, the other portion the Cumberland Coal and Iron Company and McKaig ought to pay, as they professed to own the basin; and if they would say they had no title to it, then he would pay it. I told them I could not wait, and he said the corporation ought to pay it. I talked to Mr. Humbird about it, and he said the city was not in a condition to pay it. Mr. Spates then proposed that the city should give a draft for my amount and some other amount; that he would advance the money and take a draft on the city at four months. I was anxious to get my money, so on the next Monday after the conversation between me and Col. Spates I went before the Council and made the representation. The Council then agreed to issue a draft to Col. Spates for $540, out of which he paid me. I think he paid me $440.

Ques. Look at that paper (Statement and order as to removal of boats,) and state whether you ever saw that before, and if so, under what circumstances?

Ans. In the morning before I went before the Council, Col. Spates said, "this will be our last meeting, and we had better close this thing up." Said I, "Colonel, give me something to go upon." This took place at my mill. I think this is the paper he then gave me.

Ques. In whose handwriting is it?

Ans. A part looks like my handwriting and part like Col. Spates' writing.

Ques. State what use you made of the paper?

Ans. I made up the estimate of what would be the right proportion the corporation ought to pay. I took the paper in my hand and made the statement as one of the finance committee, and the motion was made, and the order was passed levying $540. The question was asked how it should be awarded. I named Col. Alfred Spates, President Chesapeake and Ohio Canal Company. I do not remember the order being put upon that paper.

Ques. What did you do with that paper?

Ans. I left it on my desk or handed it to Mr. McKeon. It was a mere memorandum, and was not intended to be filed.

Ques. How long have you been a member of the city council?
Ans. Three years.

Ques. Was Col. Spates ever before the council for anything?
Ans. Never, to my knowledge.

Ques. Was he there on the day you made the statements?

Ans. He was not.

Ques. Was or was not the the $540 the portion the city was to pay?

Ans. It was. Col. Spates claimed the Cumberland Coal and Iron Company and McKaig ought to pay it, but as we could not make them do so, the city assumed it.

Cross-examination by Mr. Gordon.

Ques. Does your mill run altogether by water?

Ans. I have two mills. One runs altogether by water, the other—the brick mill—altogether by water, and when I have not water I run it by steam.

Ques. Where are they situated?

Ans. The flouring mill is situated 50 feet from Mechanic street on Milstead street, the other 150 feet from Mechanic street on Milstead street.

ASAHEL WILLISON.

THURSDAY, March 17th, 1870.

The Committee met at 10 o'clock, A. M., pursuant to adjournment.

Present as before.

Col. J. M. Schley.—I desire to make a statement as to how it was Mr. Spates came to make the response he did to the letter of Mr. Poe. When Mr. Spates received the letter of Mr. Poe I was called in consultation with Mr. Resley and Mr. Roman as one of his friends, and the letter of Mr. Poe was read before us. Messrs. Resley, Willison, McHenry and Lewis Smith and myself met at the Second National Bank in Cumberland the letter was laid before us by Mr. Spates, and he said, "'There is a matter, gentlemen, I desire you to look into, and I shall be guided by whatever course you dictate." After reading the letter, and a considerable consultation, we advised Mr. Spates to pursue the course which is set forth in his response to Mr. Poe's letter. The reasons we had were that we had evidence before us of the feeling of the Committee, not only in reference to Mr. Gordon, who had published the circular, but also with reference to Mr. Poe, and upon that state of facts we advised the course which was pursued by Col. Spates.

By Mr. Gordon.

Ques. What evidence had you?

Ans. I will produce that now.

Dr. WM. McPHERSON sworn.

By Mr. Schley.

Ques. Look at that paper (marked Mr. Poe's letter to Col. Spates, Nov. 8, 1869,) and state what you know of it?

Ans. I think Col. Spates showed me this letter at the Agricultural Exhibition at Cumberland.

Ques. After you saw that letter had you, or not, an interview with Mr. Poe in Cumberland, and if so, where?

Ans. I had a conversation with Mr. Poe at his room at the hotel.

Ques. State what your object was in seeing Mr. Poe?

Ans. I had no real object, except that I was interested in knowing what was the subject of investigation against Col. Spates.

Ques. Did you have any conversation with Mr. Poe in regard to these charges?

Ans. Very little conversation; nothing at all definite. Mr. told me he thought the charges were quite grave ones, without stating what they were. He said he was one of the investigators and could not communicate with me in regard to them.

Ques. Did he, or not, say to you that from the information he had, and from the gravity of the charges, he thought they were not susceptible of explanation, or words to that effect?

Ans. That was the impression left upon my mind from the conversation. I cannot recall the exact language he used.

Ques. Give the substance of that conversation by which you arrived at that conclusion, if you did arrive at that conclusion?

Ans. The substance of the conversation was that the charges were very grave and difficult of explanation, but I do not think I inferred that Mr. Poe had prejudged the case. On the contrary he rather expressed himself anxious for a fair investigation.

Cross-Examination by Mr. Poe.

Ques. Have not you and I been on quite intimate terms for a great many years?

Ans. Yes, sir.

Ques. Did you call to see me at the instance of anybody?

Ans. I did not.

Ques. How long did the interview last?

Ans. Perhaps half an hour.

Ques. When did that interview take place?

Ans. On Friday evening, Nov. 12th; just before the cars started.

Ques. Did you communicate our conversation to Col. Spates?

Ans. I met Col. Spates on the platform and told him I thought the charges were very grave from my conversation with Mr. Poe, and that Mr. Poe considered it prudent not to state what they were.

By Mr. Gordon.

Ques. Did you tell Col. Spates that Mr. Poe had prejudged the case?
Ans. I did not.

Ques. Did you have any farther conversation with Col. Spates on that subject after that time?
Ans. I did not.

Ques. Do you think what you told him could have influenced Col. Spates in writing the letter of Nov'r 16th?
Ans. I think not.

By Mr. Poe.

Ques. What language did I use in reference to my hope that Col Spates would relieve himself of these accusations?
Ans. I think you said you hoped he would have a fair investigation and that he would relieve himself.

Ques. There was not anything in that conversation from which you could infer that I had any asperity towards Col. Spates?
Ans. I think not.

W. S. McPHERSON.

Mr. Schley read the latter part of "J. H. Gorden's card," as follows:

"Now, gentlemen, if I am expected to vote for Spates in the face of these facts, I can only say that I am disappointed in the object for which you appointed me, and I cannot consent to that species of self-degradation. But I know that you had your own suspicions of his want of integrity, and that he was removed on that account; and I know that I will be sustained by you in the course I have pursued in turning out and exposing his frauds, and I shall also be sustained by you and the honest people of the State generally, in refusing to vote for him or giving him any kind of support for a place in which he, owing to the corrupt manner in which he has conducted the business heretofore entrusted to him, would only become more dangerous.

"If he was unworthy of your confidence and could not receive your votes for a place of trust, upon the report of Mr. Wailes, you surely cannot expect me to support him after the additional facts above stated have been shown.

"There are many other matters of a similar character which I might state, if it was necessary, but I will not detain you longer with these disgusting details. And now, in conclusion,

"I remain, very sincerely and truly, yours, &c.,
(Signed) "J. H. GORDON."

Gov. ODEN BOWIE sworn.

By Mr. Schley.

Ques. Look at the paper now shown to you, (marked J. H. Gordon's card,) and state whether you ever saw one of a similar purport?

Ans. No, sir. I have never seen this paper until a moment ago. I received half a dozen communications and printed forms from Mr. Gordon and others. I read one or two of them and found it was a personal quarrel, and did not read the rest. I am sure I never read this.

Ques. State whether or not you had such suspicions of Mr. Spates as are contained in that card before the election of Mr. Gordon?

Ans. I certainly had not or I would not have voted for Mr. Spates as I did on the first ballot.

Ques. State whether or not, upon those charges being made without any investigation upon both sides of the question, you sustained Mr. Gordon in opposing Mr. Spates as the nominee of the Democratic party on a mere allegation made by him?

Ans. I did not, because every man is supposed to be innocent until proven to be guilty. At the time I addressed my letter to Mr. Gordon, I was not aware that any charges had been made against Mr. Spates.

Ques. Was or was not your confidence in Mr. Spates destroyed after the report made by Mr. Wailes to the Board of Public Works?

Ans. I was never satisfied about the correctness of that report or the animus of it, and directed Mr. Wailes to submit that report to Mr. Spates.

Ques. Did you or not vote for Mr. Spates after that report was made?

Ans. I certainly voted for Mr. Spates on the first ballot. I do not recollect whether the report was made before or after the election.

Ques. Is the report of the Committee filed with the Commissioners of Public Works?

Ans. It has never been submitted to me as President of that Board. It was submitted to the general meeting of stockholders, upon the motion of Mr. Corcoran, and then the stockholders' meeting passed an order that it should be submitted to the Board of Public Works.

Ques. Did the Board of Public Works, whilst in stockholders' meeting, call upon the stockholders' meeting for the report?

Ans. No, sir.

Ques. Do you know how it was that Mr. Corcoran happened to call for that report?

Ans. I do not.

Ques. After the election of Colonel Spates as Senator from Allegany county, did not Mr. Poe have an interview with you in the city of Baltimore with reference to these charges against Col. Spates?

Ans. I do not know that it was with reference to the charges; it was a mere casual interview. We met in the counting-room of J. P. Pleasants & Sons in Baltimore. I left the counting-room and Mr. Poe came out after me, and said that, as he had informed another member of the Board of Public Works about these charges, he felt it his duty to tell me of certain charges against Mr. Spates. He did not tell me anything like the number of charges that were made in that report. I was in a hurry, and the whole conversation did not last three minutes.

Ques. What response did you make to Mr. Poe?

Ans. I do not recollect, except that I was on important business and had no time then.

Ques. State whether or not you did not say to Mr. Poe that you knew nothing about that, and did not want to be informed in reference to it?

Ans. No, sir; I am sure I did not say that.

Ques. Do you recollect saying, when he said he had talked to another member of the Board, that you supposed that was Mr. Fowler?

Ans. Yes; I did say that.

Ques. Did you want to hear anything about that?

Ans. I certainly did not at that time, because I had not the time. I did not want to hear anything about it outside of the Board of Public Works.

Ques. State to the Committee whether or not you had an interview with Mr. Gordon in his room at Mrs. Green's, and, if you had, how you came to go into his room?

Ans. I had an interview with Mr. Gordon, at his request, about the last of November or first of December, in his room at Mrs. Green's. Mr. Gordon asked me into his room after dinner; said he felt it his duty to communicate to me the fact of this investigation into the management of the Canal Company, and certain transactions connected with it.

Ques. Was that after the election of Mr. Spates?

Ans. It was.

Ques. Do you recollect what he said?

Ans. In substance he told me they had discovered some corrupt transactions on the part of Mr. Spates. The conversation was quite a short one, and he did not enter into particulars.

Ques. Did he or not, at that or any other time, consult you as to whether it would not be right for him, Gordon, to initiate some proceedings to prevent Mr. Spates from taking his seat in the Senate?

Ans. Mr. Gordon asked whether some proceedings ought not to be taken to prevent Mr. Spates from taking his seat in the Senate if these charges were true. I replied that was a matter I had nothing to do with, and did not want to give any advice; that it was a matter for the action of the Senate.

Ques. State whether or not you were applied to by a reporter to give your consent to the publication of this report of the Committee to the stockholder's meeting, and whether or not you refused?

Ans. I was applied to at the executive mansion on the day of the stockholder's meeting, whilst at dinner, by Mr. McGarrigell, of the American, and Mr. Fawcett. Mr. McGarrigell asked me to give the press of Baltimore, for publication, the report of this Committee made to the stockholder's meeting. I told them the report was not in my possession; that it was not in the possession of the Board of Public Works, and that I had never seen it, and only heard it read that day.

Ques. Did you refuse your consent to its publication?
Ans. I had nothing to do with it. My consent was not asked.

Ques. Did you make the remark that they had better let that alone?
Ans. I think I did.

Ques. Did Fawcett say anything to you?
Ans. Fawcett said he had come along with McGarrigell at Mr. Gordon's direction to know whether McGarrigell could have the report. If the report had been in my possession I would not have given it to the press for publication until I had given Mr. Spates an opportunity to vindicate himself.

Cross-Examination by Mr. Gordon.

Ques. In regard to the conversation at Mrs. Green's, did not I state to you that I had been urged very much to institute criminal proceedings against Mr. Spates?
Ans. You did.

Ques. Was it not the object of my interview to consult you in regard to my duty as President of the Company in the matter?
Ans. I think it was. You told me you felt it your duty to tell me all this. I said, with reference to the proceedings in the Senate, it was a matter entirely with the Senate, and I thought the Canal Board had nothing to do with it.

Ques. Was there anything to prevent my bringing charges in the Senate?
Ans. There was nothing to prevent it, or any other man from bringing such charges.

By Mr. Poe.

Ques. Do you happen to know whether or not the report made by Wailes in reference to this boat building had or had not any influence upon the mind of any member of the Board of Public Works in reference to the election of Mr. Spates?
Ans. I do not believe it had.

ODEN BOWIE.

R. M. Sprigg recalled.

By Mr. Schley.

Ques. In what capacity is Neil Burston connected with the canal?

Ans. As boss carpenter.

Ques. Is it his business to make purchases of lumber?

Ans. He purchased the lumber and reported it to me, and I set it down in my book.

Ques. Do you know of your own knowledge of the purchase and exchange of this lumber and iron with Col. Spates?

Ans. I do.

Ques. Where was the lumber and iron gotten?

Ans. From Col. Spates' yard.

Ques. What kind of lumber was it?

Ans. Heavy dry oak lumber, that I could not get anywhere else.

Ques. State the amount of iron you got from him, and when you got it?

Ans. In August, 1867, I got $20 worth, and also sent to the tunnel $70 worth. In February, 1868, I got 2250 pounds at 5 cents, $112.50; in March, 1800 pounds, $90.00, and 1650 pounds $82.50, in all $375.00 worth.

Ques. Did you get any lumber yourself?

Ans. I did not. The amount Berston reported to me of lumber and iron gotten by him is $750.00.

Ques. How do you know that this iron came from Col. Spates' yard?

Ans. I saw drays hauling the iron out of Col. Spates' yard, and the Canal Company's hands were with the drays loading them.

Ques. Has it not always been customary on your Division to make exchanges of lumber?

Ans. It is a common practice to make such exchanges.

Ques. Has it not been done since Mr. Gordon became President of the Company?

Ans. It has. Berston has made exchanges since they turned me off. He was making an exchange with John Suyder, the boat builder, at the time they went down on the packet.

Cross-Examination by Mr. Gordon.

Ques. You say you got some iron from Mr. Spates in August, 1867. What sort of iron was it?

Ans. One and a-half inch round iron. Some of the bars were 18 and some 20 feet long. All of it was heavy round iron.

Ques. What was it used for?

Ans. For repairs on the Canal.

Ques. When was the iron you got in August, 1867, used, and for what purpose the $20 and $70 worth?

Ans. In January, 1868, some of it was used for pinning cribs together.

Ques. Was it returned on your abstract for January, 1868?

Ans. Yes, sir.

Ques. For what was that $112.50 worth used you received in February, 1868?

Ans. For repairing locks, cribs, &c.

Ques. When was that returned?

Ans. In February, 1868.

Ques. What did you do with the iron you got in March, 1868?

Ans. That was used in February, 1869.

Ques. Was that returned in your abstract for February, 1869?

Ans. Yes, and a great deal other iron was returned besides that.

Ques. How did you return it?

Ans. I weighed the iron, and whatever it was worth, put it in the summary.

Ques. Had you any bill for it?

Ans. No, sir. I returned it with the repairs as a part of my expenses.

Ques. Did you get allowed for it?

Ans. Yes, sir.

Ques. Did you get allowed for all your expenses returned on your abstract?

Ans. Yes, sir, I think I did.

Ques. What kind of work were you doing in February and March, 1867?

Ans. Cleaning the Canal and repairing all over the Division.

Ques. What amount of repairs did the lock at Old Town require?

Ans. Over a thousand dollars' worth. We tore it down and rebuilt it.

Ques. Did you rebuild any others?

Ans. We repaired all that needed it.

Ques. Were any other locks repaired and rebuilt in January, 1869?

Ans. The principal part of the repairing on locks was done in that month. I do not recollect how many we did.

Ques. What other work did you do in those months?

Ans. We cleaned out the bars, and all work that was necessary.

Ques. What kind of work did you do in the December previous?

Ans. We repaired a good many locks and other work.

Ques. What carpenters had you on your Division in 1868?

Ans. Berston, Noonan, Brinker, Smeltzer and William Wineow worked at Cumberland.

Ques. Who kept their time?

Ans. Berston did of his hands.

Ques. Are you sure all that iron was returned on those abstracts?

Ans. I cannot tell certainly. Some of it may have gone in some other time, but I think it went in the abstracts for those months.

Ques. If you returned it and got paid for it, how could you have exchanged it with Col. Spates for lumber?

Ans. I do not recollect how it was done now. It has been a good while ago.

Ques. You say you got part of that iron in August, 1867, and part in February and March, 1868; how could you exchange that iron for lumber that was not bought until September, 1868?

Ans. I got the iron and took it away, and was going to buy it, but afterwards, instead of paying for it, I paid Mr. Bruce for the lumber Mr. Spates got.

Ques. Look at your abstract for January, 1868, and show us how that iron was returned?

Ans. It is not returned here at all.

Ques. Look at your abstract for February, 1868?

Ans. It is not returned here either.

Ques. Is it in your abstract for February, 1869, now shown you?

Ans. It is not returned in this one.

Ques. Can you tell us where it has been returned then?

Ans It has not been returned if it is not on the abstract.

Ques. Who kept the time of the laboring hands on the canal?

Ans. The bosses.

Ques. Who was the boss at Cumberland?

Ans. Terrell was from the time I went on until the spring of 1869.

Ques. Had you any masons that worked during that time?

Ans. Yes.

Ques. Who kept their time?

Ans. They kept it themselves.

Ques. What were they at work at?

Ans. Different kinds of work; on the culvert, water break, fixing the stop lock, getting out stone for the waste way, &c.

Ques. Who were they?

Ans. James Mulligan and Patrick Kennedy.

Ques. Did they do any other work in the fall of 1868?

Ans. I do not think they worked for me after August.

Ques. What carpenters had you at work at that time?

Ans. That is more than I can tell.

Ques. Did they make constant time?

Ans. Pretty much.

Ques. Did not they do some work for Col. Spates?

Ans. They did for a few days.

Ques. Did you pay them for that work?

Ans. I think I did return it to the Company. I paid them for the time they worked.

Ques. What work did they do?

Ans. They may be framed a carriage house, but did not build it.

R. M. SPRIGG.

Philip J. Cahill sworn.

By Mr. Gordon.

Where do you reside?

Ans. In Cumberland.

Ques. What is your business?

Ans. Clerk for Henry Thomas Weld, at his boat yard in Cumberland.

Ques. Where is Mr. Weld's boat yard as compared with that of the Chesapeake and Ohio Canal?

Ans. Just across the basin. The Company's yard is on one side of the lock, ours is directly opposite. From shore to shore the distance is about ninety feet.

Ques. Do you recollect of Mr. Weld doing some work for the Chesapeake and Ohio Canal Company on an ice breaker in 1867?

Ans. Yes, sir.

Ques. Where was that done?

Ans. In the upper end of our yard next to the basin.

Ques. By whose hands was this work done?

Ans. By the hands of both parties.

Ques. State the hands of Mr. Weld who worked on that boat, and how long each man worked on it?

Mr. Schley objected to this testimony as simply a matter of veracity between Mr. Sheridan and Mr. Sprigg, and not pertinent to the issue.

Mr. Gordon proposed to examine Mr. Cahill for the purpose of showing that Sheridan's statements in regard to these receipts were correct, and that the receipts were filled up for more time than Mr. Cahill had given to Mr. Sprigg, as the time of the men that worked on those boats, and that Sprigg received more money than he was entitled to.

Mr. Schley replied that there was no controversy in reference to that item in any of the charges set forth in the report of the Committee.

The Committee decided that the testimony of Mr. Cahill for such a purpose was irrevelent, on the ground that the subject was a collateral matter, and the testimony of Mr. Sprigg had been brought out on Mr. Gordon's examination, and therefore he was bound by his answers.

By Mr. Gordon.

Ques. How long have you been employed with Mr. Weld?

Ans. Since June, 1858.

Ques. Have you been there constantly?

Ans. I have been away eight months.

Ques. Have you had a great deal of intercourse with the boat builders?

Ans. Generally I know them, but am confined to the office.

Ques. Did you ever know a man named Thomas Sheridan, a "boat builder?"

Ans. None, except Sheridan in Weld's yard.

Ques. Is the boat building confined to the river and canal at Cumberland?

Ans. It is.

Cross-Examination by Mr. Schley.

Ques. Are you in the habit of going over to the boat yard of the Canal Company?

Ans. Not often; occasionally.

Ques. Might there not have been a Tom Sheridan building a boat without your knowing it?

Ans. It is possible, but I do not think it very likely.

Ques. Do you know whether there were any boats built on Wills creek?

Ans. I remember when there were, about ten years ago. The yard was afterwards filled up.

Ques. Do you remember that a boat was built there after the channel was filled up with sand and that a channel was cut in the sand for the purpose of getting the boat out?

Ans. I remember the opening of a channel for some purpose. I do not know whether for getting a boat out or not?

By Mr. Gordon.

Ques. How long ago was that?
Ans. I think it was before the war.

P. J. CAHILL.

JAMES NOONAN recalled.

By Mr. Gordon.

Ques. Did you work for the Canal Company in October and November, 1867, at Cumberland?

Ans. Yes, sir. I worked on the ice breakers, lock gates, &c., and in the shop.

Ques. How many ice breakers were built for the Company that fall, and where were they built?

Ans. Three. One on Weld's yard and two on the Company's yard.

Ques. Who built those boats?
Ans. The Company's hands.

Ques. Who was the foreman?
Ans. Mr. Berston.

Ques. Was there a man named Sheridan at work on any of those boats?

Ans. Not on any of those we helped to build.

Ques. Did you ever know any such boat builder?
Ans. I did not.

Ques. Did you ever hear of any such person?
Ans. I did.

Ques. Where was he?
Ans. He worked in town.

Ques. There was a man by the name of Sheridan, Superintendent for Weld. Did you ever know any other Thomas Sheridan, a boat builder?

Ans. I did not know him.

Ques. What lumber did you build those boats out of?
Ans. It was furnished by the Company.

Cross-Examination.

Ques. Were there any hands working on those boats except the Company's hands?

Ans. There were.

Ques. Were there any that you did not know?

Ans. There were men that I did not know, but none of those that worked in the Company's yard that I did not know.

By Mr. Clarke.

Ques. What were the names of the men who worked on the boats with you?

Ans. Brinker, Apple, Smeltzer, Wineow, Berston and myself.

By Mr. Poe.

Ques. Do you know of any man undertaking to direct the work as foreman on either of those boats you helped to build, except Mr. Berston?

Ans. No, sir.

By Mr. Spates.

Ques. You worked on one of the boats in the Company's yard, and on the boat built in Weld's yard. Those were the only boats on which you worked were they not?

Ans. Yes, sir.

Ques. And the men working on those boats were the ones you knew?

Ans. Yes, sir.

Ques. Were there not other men working on the other boat that you did not know?

Ans. Yes, sir.

By Mr. Gordon.

Ques. You did not work on both boats at the same time?

Ans. No, sir.

Ques. Were you called away at the time the boats were building?

Ans. Yes; several days at a time.

Ques. Where was the other boat building?

Ans. Above the carpenter shop.

Ques. Was that building at the same time you were at work on the boat in Weld's yard?

Ans. About the same time.

Ques. How far were they apart?

Ans. I could not exactly tell the distance.

By Mr. Clarke.

Ques. You said you had heard of another Sheridan; from whom did you hear of him?

Ans. I heard Mr. Sprigg speak of him. Mr. Sprigg was in a hurry with the boats, and told me he would give one of them out at contract, and said he had set a man named Sheridan to work on it.

Being recalled at my own request, I desire to correct my testimony as to the three ice breakers. I only worked on two of them—one built between the flume and the shop, and the other in Weld's yard in the year 1867.

JAMES NOONAN.

FRIDAY, March 18th, 1870.

The Committee met at 9½ o'clock A. M., pursuant to adjournment.

Present as before.

CASPER BRINKER sworn.

By Mr. Gordon.

Ques. Where did you live in the months of October and November, 1867?

Ans. In Cumberland.

Ques. For whom did you work?

Ans. For Fred. Merton & Snyder.

Ques. For whom did you work in the month of November?

Ans. Most of the time for the Canal Company. I was sent there by Mr. Snyder, and worked on the ice breaker that was built in Weld's yard.

Ques. When did you commence working on it?

Ans. I am not certain about the time; I think from the 18th to the 20th of November, 1867.

Ques. Who paid you for that work?

Ans. Fred. Merton paid me.

Ques. Where were the three ice breakers built?

Ans. One was built between the shop and the flume, the other was built in Weld's yard, and the third I know nothing about.

Ques. Who worked with you on those ice breakers?

Mr. Schley objected to farther testimony in regard to the ice breakers, because it was not rebutting testimony.

Mr. Gordon said he proposed to show that these ice breakers were built by the Company's hands, who were returned by Mr. Sprigg on his abstract and paid for by him, and that no such man as Thomas Sheridan worked on those boats.

The Committee sustained the objection, upon the ground that it was not rebutting testimony; that the same subject had been inquired into, without restriction by the Committee, in the examination-in-chief.

CASPER BRINKER.

Dr. J. J. Bruce recalled.

By Mr. Gordon.

Ques. Is the statement made by Mr. Sprigg in his evidence correct, that he and Col. Spates came in your office and he had a conversation with you at the time Col. Spates paid you $1,052.60?

Ans. It is entirely incorrect. Neither he nor anybody else was present, and Col. Spates paid me only $252.60.

Ques Have you refreshed your memory in regard to that matter by looking at your books?

Mr. Schley objected to the introduction of books at this time, that being new and independent proof, and not rebutting testimony, and the objection was sustained by the Committee. *

By Mr. Poe.

Ques. Have you taken into consideration the contradiction of your testimony by Mr. Sprigg? Have you fully considered it, and is your recollection of it affected by anything Mr. Sprigg has said?

Ans. My recollection is perfectly clear on the subject. My first statement is true.

J. J. BRUCE.

Francis Smeltzer recalled.

By Mr. Gordon.

Ques. Where were the four loads of lumber unloaded you spoke of?

Ans. Opposite Mr. Willard's office, at the back of Gephart's watch house.

Ques. How far is that from Mr. Tasker's house?

Ans. Just across the street.

---

* Note by Committee.—The grounds on which the Committee sustained the objection to the testimony of J. J. Bruce are not fully stated above. Mr. Bruce's testimony had been to some extent contradicted by the testimony of Sprigg, and the Committee were of opinion that as Bruce had been examined in chief in regard to the same subject matter, he ought to have refreshed his memory before he testified, and that it was not competent for him, as a rebutting witness, to sustain his own testimony in chief, or to introduce books for that purpose which were not evidence, per se, and which being in his possession he could have produced for the purpose of refreshing his memory on his examination-in-chief.

Ques. Was the lumber all unloaded upon one day, or how many days were you unloading it?

Objected to by Mr. Schley as not being rebutting testimony.

The Committee decided that while the questions would have been proper upon the cross examination of the witness when he was before upon the stand, while the Committee would have allowed him to have been recalled at any time before the testimony for the defense had closed for the purpose of allowing his further cross-examination, that since the defense has closed its testimony and the further examination is objected to by counsel for the defense, the Committee are of opinion that it is not rebutting testimony.

FRANCIS SMELTZER.

BENJAMIN FAWCETT recalled.

By Mr. Poe.

Ques. When you were first examined you stated that the endorsement "voucher No. 54," and "voucher No. 55," on the Tasker bills were in Mr. Peck's handwriting. Were you in error?

Mr. Schley—I object.

Mr. Poe waived the question.

Ques. Were you present at the Board when the report of Mr. Sprigg of December, 1868, came in?

Ans. Yes, sir.

Ques. Who brought it?

Ans. Col. Spates brought it and presented it to the Board.

Ques. Were there any vouchers of any kind with it?

Ans. I never saw any.

Ques. Were the two Tasker bills of $1,200 and $150 which have been produced in evidence, the only papers purporting to have been executed by that firm for those amounts, ever filed in the office to your knowledge?

Ans. The only papers for those amounts ever filed in the office to my knowledge.

Ques. Look at the abstracts of R. M. Sprigg for September and October, 1868, and state when they were received at the office?

Ans. The September abstract was received on the 13th of October, the other on the 16th of October.

Ques. Were they taken out of the office to your knowledge at any time?

Ans. They were.

Ques. How long were they out of the office?
Ans. From three weeks to a month.
Objected to by Mr. Schley as not being rebutting testimony.
The Committee sustained the objection.

BENJ. FAWCETT.

FRIDAY, March 18th, 1870.

The Committee met at 4½ o'clock, P. M., pursuant to adjournment. Present as before.

Mr. Poe said: When we had offered the *prima facie* testimony, my inclination and judgment was that it was becoming in me to retire from this case, and I would have done so, if it had not been that the course of examination on the part of Mr. Schley showed that there was going to be a conflict of testimony and an attack upon witnesses upon whom we relied, and I felt it my duty to take part in the proceedings for the purpose of seeing that justice was done to them; but I do not consider myself under any obligation to remain for the purpose of doing any more to aid the Committee in the prosecution of its labors. I feel uncomfortable in the appearance of being here to urge the Committee by insisting upon the production of evidence which they do not seem to think is relevant or competent, and perhaps I agree in their decisions in regard to some of the testimony. On the whole I consider that I have done my duty, and I am not inclined of my own motion to go any farther, but I will say this in justice to the *prima facie* case—to our testimony up to the time Mr. Schley commenced his defense—that in the experience I have had of cases in which witnesses have been examined at different times, I have known no case in which the testimony came so completely up to the expectation and to the previous experience of the testimony, with the solitary exception of one witness, as in this case; and I desire to be understood as saying that, in my humble judgment, up to that point the case was as completely established as a *prima facie* case could be. I say not one word as to the effect of the testimony that has been offered on the other side. I have my decided convictions about it, but that is for the Committee to determine; but in making this remark I hope I may not be considered as intimating any sort of doubt of being able to sustain the position we took in that report.

Mr. Gordon said: I have no disposition to remain, except to vindicate my own position, and as Mr. Poe has said, witnesses were brought here in conflict with other witnesses, and I thought it my duty to see that justice is done as far as possible. I shall bow to the will of the Committee, and only take part to see that witnesses are protected, and that the Committee gets full and fair statements of facts in the case. We have permitted a great deal of testimony to go in which is not relevant, and we only stand here for the purpose of seeing that justice is done as far as possible.

Mr. Clarke asked that a summons be issued for Sidney J. Wailes, Paymaster of the Chesapeake and Ohio Canal Company, to appear before the Committee for slandering and traducing the Committee which was so ordered.

JUDGE J. VEIRS BOUIC sworn.

By *Mr. Gordon.*

Ques. Were you a director of the Canal Company in 1868?

Ans. I was, sir.

Ques. Do you know anything of a report that was sent into the Canal Company's office from the Superintendent of the Cumberland Division in December, 1868?

Ans. There was such a report sent in that was read, from my recollection, at the January meeting, 1869, at the table of the directors.

Ques. Were there any vouchers or receipts accompanying that report?

Ans. I have no recollection to have seen any.

Ques. State whether you have any knowledge of the cause which brought that report?

Ans. My recollection is that, at the meeting of the Board on the 1st of November or the 1st of December, I am not positive which, what was usually termed by the Board the estimates for the month from the several Superintendents, were laid before the Board. These estimates were the foundation upon which the Superintendents drew the money to pay their expenditure for the previous month for work on their Divisions. When the amount asked for by the Superintendent of the Cumberland Division was read, it struck me as being larger than usual; however, there was nothing in it "so remarkable as to attract my attention very especially to it, but when we went to adjourn the order was passed, to my recollection, that drafts should be issued to the Superintendents for the amounts that they asked for, and it was passed without any particular examination of the return or of these estimates." I said, "Perhaps we had better look into these reports before the drafts are issued." But it was remarked by some member of the Board, "We can do that when we come from dinner," or "We can do it to-morrow." I said I did not expect to stay here to-morrow, and I am not sure that I can come back this afternoon. After we got dinner I found that I had time to go back to the office, and either at the office or on the way there, I said something to Mr. Fawcett about the expenses being larger than usual, as it occurred to me from memory. He then said that that was occasioned by items for new boats on the several Divisions being put in the returns. No quorum of the Board appearing, I told Mr. Fawcett if the directors came to ask them to look into that matter to see whether there was not some error about it before the drafts went out, and then started home. I was apprehensive of paying for the boats twice. My recollection was that the boats were to be built at Cumberland, out of material of the Company, and that the work was to be done by employees of the Company.

Mr. Schley—I object to all this testimony. There has been no estimate offered here. An estimate is one thing and an abstract another.

Witness—I will here explain that the paper I spoke of was simply a list of expenditures made by the Superintendent, which I always contended was no estimate, but, in the language of the Board, it was called an estimate. The mode of doing business, when I was in the Board, was that the Superintendent returned a paper containing a list of items of expenditures, which he called his estimate, but in fact it was his statement of items of expenditure which had been made previous to his return. The Board meeting in December would receive a list of expenditures for what had been spent in the month preceding the meeting. The Superintendent did not ask us to put money into his hands to incur liabilities, but to pay off the liabilities that had been incurred during the preceding month.

Mr. Gordon—What was done about this matter?

Ans. When this list of expenditures, to use my own language, was laid before the Board at the meeting of the 1st of December, the amounts, from memory, struck me as being larger than was usual, and following up that impression I commenced inquiries of which I have spoken, and Mr. Fawcett said that it was because of items being put in on the several Divisions for building the boats.

Mr. Schley—I object to what Mr. Fawcett said?

Mr. Gordon—Had you a conversation with Mr. Spates?

Ans. I had to leave, and when I returned I made farther inquiries about what had been done in that matter; and then I examined the papers myself, either in connection with Mr. Fawcett or Mr. Peck, and discovered items of expenditure for cost of boats for Mr. Maus and other Superintendents for whom boats had been ordered to be built. I then directed the clerks to make out extracts from the vouchers and returns of Mr. Sprigg, showing the materials and labor that had been employed by him in building these boats as far as they appeared upon the records, and when the Board met I had prepared a draft of a resolution looking to having the matter inquired into, and was going to call the attention of the Board to it. Mr. Spates walked around to where I was sitting, and asked me what I was driving at. I got up and said I wanted to have some explanation about these items for boats. He said "What about that?" and I said "It seems to me that these boats had been paid for twice." He told me I was laboring under a mistake, and although it seemed to be so, that these returns had been made in order to equalize the expenditures of the several Divisions, and went on to give explanations that looked reasonable. I then replied to him that "All I am after is to have this thing right on our records." He said it should be put right. I told him I did not see there was anything wrong about it. He said Mr. Sprigg would make all that right, and he would see that an explanatory return was made which would be satisfactory, and I said " Very well, I won't offer the resolution," and there the matter ended.

Before the meeting of the Board I had got matter from the books from which it appeared to me that my first impression was correct. I sat down and wrote a letter to the Committee on Accounts.

ROCKVILLE, Dec. 23, '68.

MESSRS. THOMAS & PICKEREL:

Dear Sirs :—It seems to me that the amount of money spent on the Cumberland Division in excess of the expenditures on the other Divisions requires great scrutiny on your part, as the Committee on Accounts, into the disbursements on that Division.

If you carefully examine his (Sprigg's) accounts for September and October, you will find :

```
Sept. New Scow for Shay.............................................  $800 00
      Do.     for G. W. Spates....................................   800 00
      Materials for new House Boat for Spates..............   300 00
                                                                     ─────────
                                                                     $1,900 00
Oct. New Scows—Materials— J. Bruce's Bill......$1,257 10
     J. H. Dubant & Son...........................   34 40
     W. Dow & Son...................................   40 00
     Lefever & Son....................................   72 36
     H. P. Tasker & Sons............................  293 17
                                                     ─────────
                                                     $1,697 03
                                                                     $2,161 03
Oct. Paid on Scows by I. R. Mans..................  $400 00
                     by John Shay..................   600 00
                     by G. W. Spates.............. 1,200 00
                                                     ─────────
                                                                    $2,200 00
```

Whole cost of the three Boats is............................$6,261 03

This amount of money has been *paid out* on *the drafts* of Sprigg for these boats alone, as shown by the vouchers, except the $2,200 which is paid by Messrs. Spates and Shay. Col. Spates stated to me he would cause this matter to be put right on *our records*, which I presume he will do.

But I shall insist on our records showing exactly what these boats cost, and to whom, and for what the money has been paid. I shall therefore insist that you, as Financial Committee, shall *report* to our Board the cost of these boats, and therein show how much lumber has been used in these boats and what it cost; also how much iron and other items of material were used, and what it cost; how much labor was employed, and what it cost. I shall insist that you scrutinize the bills for materials of every kind, so that none be allowed as a credit on account of these boats that was not in fact used in building them.

And if you have any doubts on this subject, it is an easy matter for you to order the boats to be measured by a competent man, and the quantity of materials thus accurately ascertained.

And you have a right also to call to your aid the Clerk and Assistant Clerk of our Board, to enable you to make an accurate statement and report on this subject. Yours, &c.,

W. VEIRS BOUIC.

By Mr. Gordon—State whether the letter now shown to you (marked Judge Bouic's letter), is the one which you wrote?

Ans. It is.

Ques. Do the items which you speak of here, correspond with the papers as they were in the office?

Ans. That is my recollection of the fact; that I wrote that letter from data which I had obtained from returns in the office, and at the time I obtained it.

By Mr. Schley—Who did you get those returns from?

Ans. My recollection is that I first called on Mr. Fawcett for them and that he either sent me to Mr. Peck's room, or that we went together; but I would not undertake to say from which office I got the returns from. The extracts were in Mr. Fawcett's handwriting.

By Mr. Gordon—Did the items correspond with the papers in the office?

Ans. That is my recollection, that those items corresponded with what I had seen on the papers in the office. I believed them to be the same when I wrote.

By Mr. Clarke—From what books did you take these items?

Ans. I would not repeat that I took them from books. I called on the clerks to show me the evidences or the vouchers by which I could see what expenditures had been made, and they produced vouchers or papers, and showed them to me. I looked over them casually, and directed them to make the extracts I needed, and relied upon the information they gave me. I had not the time to devote to an examination of the papers. When I wanted information I would go to the clerks and ask them for it, and when they gave it to me, I took it for granted that it was correct.

After the occasion that I have spoken of, and after I had written this letter, which substantially recites what I have stated, I went to a meeting of the Board, and, as was usual, the reports of the several Divisions were called for and read, and amongst others a report from the Cumberland Division. After it was read, and my mind not being able to perceive that that report attained the object for which it was intended, and having a conviction that there was an error, I made the motion, which was intended to accomplish the purpose for which I had written the letter, to refer the report to the Committee on Accounts. I had no means of knowing that the report was correct, and not having the time to examine it, I wanted to be satisfied that there were no errors before voting to appropriate the amount of money called for.

Mr. Gordon—I offer Mr. Sprigg's estimate for September for the purpose of showing that Mr. Sprigg in that report, filed on the 31st of December, either did not refer to his estimate for September, or else his report is not correct.

Mr. Schley—I object, because it is a new paper which has not been introduced into the examination in chief, or upon the cross-examination.

Mr. Gordon—I offer it also in connection with Judge Bowie's testimony, to show that these items could not have been taken from that paper.

Objection sustained by the Committee.

Mr. Gordon—In response to what Mr. Poe has said, although I do not agree that he has made out a *prima facie* case, I desire to state that I appreciate the motive that seems to actuate him from this time out—that he has simply discharged his duty, and has got to that point from which he does not feel called upon to press home with the Committee the charges, and he has carried out his determination since he made the remark.

Mr. Spates—I also appreciate what Mr. Poe has said highly, and shall remember it with gratitude.

Mr. Poe—I hope that no inference will be drawn from anything that I have said, that the testimony has abated in the slightest degree my confidence in the report of the Committee of Accounts.

Mr. Schley—I desire to say in reply, that the more vigor with which you prosecute your case, the better I will like it. I ask no quarter at your hands. I do not want you to say one thing and do another, and hope you will push home every point you have with all the energy in your power.

SATURDAY, March 19, 1870.

The Committee met at 9 o'clock.

Present—Messrs. Henry, (Chairman,) and Clarke.

LLOYD LOWE sworn.

By Mr. Gordon.

Ques. Where do you reside?

Ans. In Cumberland.

Ques. How long have you lived there?

Ans. Ten years in Cumberland.

Ques. What has been your business?

Ans. Part of the time I was on the Canal as Superintendent?

Ques. Have you been pretty familiar with the Canal on that Division.

Ans. Yes.

Ques. Look at the abstract of Mr. Sprigg for September.

Ans. It is all in my handwriting except the statement where the paper is pasted on.

Ques. Was Mr. Sprigg present when it was made out?

Ans. Yes.

Mr. Schley objected to the testimony and his objection was sustained by the Committee as not being rebutting testimony.

Ques. Look at the abstract of R. M. Sprigg for December, 1868? What that abstract made out by Mr. Sprigg's direction?

Ans. It was.

Ques. Was he present when that was made out.

Ans. He was.

LLOYD LOWE.

J. T. Blackistone, Sergeant-at-Arms of the Senate, who had been directed to summon N. J. Berston as a witness before the Committee, returned this morning and reported as follows:

I met Mr. Berston on the street, in Cumberland, whilst on my way to his house to summon him. He said he was only able to get out for the first time for some time to attend to some little business. He seemed to be very much fatigued from shortness of breath and had to sit down whilst I was talking to him. I served the summons on him, and he said he would love to come to Annapolis, but that his health was in such a condition that he believed it would kill him if he did so. My own conviction was that he was not in a condition to come. I afterwards, at the hotel, saw Dr. Dougherty, who represented himself to be his family physician. He (the doctor) expressed the opinion that he could go without detriment to his health. I then requested him to reduce his opinion to writing, stating that I disliked to take the responsibility of bringing a man here at the peril of his life. He declined to give any written statement to that effect. I then, feeling anxious to discharge my duty, went again in pursuit of the witnesss. I found him seated in a store where there were quite a number of gentlemen present, among them Dr. Geo. C. Perry. After recapitulating the conversation, which occurred between Dr. Dougherty and myself, to him, he insisted that he could not come without endangering his life—having to come into a strange place and go into a room in which he had been unaccustomed to sleeping. I then told him he would have to get the certificate of some physician as to his condition. Dr. Perry, who was present, remarked that there could be no difficulty about that, for that he was clearly of opinion that his health was such that his health was such that it would really endanger his life to go down, whereupon I asked him to reduce to writing his opinion, which he did, and which I return to the Committee:

CUMBERLAND, March 16, 1870.

To the Hon. T. Blackiston.

It is my candid opinion as a physician that if Mr. Neal Berston is removed to Annapolis it will be the death him. He is not in a condition to be taken from home.

(Signed,)   GEO. C. PERRY, M. D.

The Committee then ordered that the testimony of N. J. Berston be taken before a Justice of the Peace, at Cumberland, in the presence of both parties, or their counsel, if they chose to be present, and ruled out an *ex parte* affidavit offered in evidence by Mr. Schley.

Theodore W. Evans sworn.

By Mr. Gordon.

Ques. Were you in the employment of Tasker & Co. in the fall of 1868?

Ans. Yes, sir.

Ques. In what capacity.

Ans. As clerk in the store.

Ques. Had you any duties to perform in connection with the lumber business?

Ans. None, sir.

Ques. Did you assist or have anything to do with the unloading of four car loads of lumber for the Canal Company?

Ans. No, sir.

Ques. Do you know of any four car loads of lumber for the Canal Company from Tasker & Co.'s?

Ans. I know of but one load of lumber, and that was received on a double truck, for the Canal Company.

Ques. Where was that unloaded?

Ans. Across from the depot, back of Gephart's little watch house.

Ques. Can you see that switch from the window of your counting room?

Ans. Yes, sir; it is not over forty or fifty yards distant.

Ques. Do you know of any other lumber that was sold to the Canal Company?

Ans. No, sir; nothing more than what I saw on the books.

Cross-Examined by Mr. Schley.

Ques. Do you know to whom all lumber goes that is unloaded there by Gephart's?

Ans. I do not know to whom all the lumber is consigned. There is a great deal of lumber unloaded there.

Ques. Might there not have been more car loads of lumber for the Canal Company unloaded there and you not know it?

Ans. Yes, sir.

By Mr. Gordon.

Ques. Is it likely that there would have been four car loads of lumber from Tasker & Co.'s house unloaded there and you not have known it?

Ans. It is likely I would have known something about it.

T. W. EVANS.

W. R. McCulley recalled.

By Mr. Gordon.

Ques. Do you know anything of four car loads of lumber unloaded from the house of Tasker & Co. at the little switch back of Gephart's, in the fall of 1868, for the Canal Company?

Ans. No, sir.

Ques. How far is that from the window of your office, and can you see that place from the window?

Ans. Yes, sir. It is diagonally across the street.

Ques. Is it likely that those four car loads could have been delivered and you not know it?

Ans. I should think not. The entries would necessarily have to be made by me.

Ques. How long would it take to unload 40,000 or 50,000 feet of lumber?

Ans. I do not know.

Cross-Examination.

Ques. You only know of the lumber that was returned to you?

Ans. Yes, sir.

Ques. Is not that switch by Gephart's the point where the majority of the lumber is unloaded?

Ans. Some of it was taken down opposite to the yards.

Ques. Did you notice the marks on the cars whenever you passed them?

Ans. I did not.

W. R. McCULLEY.

H. P. TASKER recalled.

By Mr. Gordon.

Ques. Mr. Smeltzer stated in his testimony that he helped to unload four car loads of lumber which was gotten for the Canal Company from your house in Cumberland, and that it was unloaded on the little switch back of Gephart's watch-house, in the fall of 1868. Was there any such four loads of lumber gotten by the Canal Company in that fall?

Ans. There was not.

Ques. Does the railroad company permit lumber to stand on that switch for any length of time?

Ans. I have known cars to stand there a day or two. They could not put on that switch at one time more than two gondolas or more than one pair of trucks. The only lumber for the Canal Company came on a pair of trucks.

Ques. Do you know whether the Canal Company has any place in their yard for 40,000 or 50,000 feet of lumber, and have room enough for building boats at the same time?

Ans. I do not know.

Cross-Examination by Mr. Schley.

Ques. When lumber comes there do they not haul it away at once?

Ans. Yes, sir.

Ques. Has the Canal Company got room in their yard to pile 40,000 feet of lumber?

Ans. I do not know.

Ques. Can you pile it on a half acre of ground?

Ans. It can be piled on less than that.

By Mr. Gordon.

Ques. If the half acre was covered by other things you could not?

Ans. No, sir.

By Mr. Schley.

Ques. Suppose you had an acre and a quarter?
Ans. That would hold a good deal of lumber.
Ques. What amount of lumber have you ever received on one car?
Ans. The most I have ever gotten down on one car is 8,000 feet.

H. P. TASKER.

LLOYD LOWE recalled.

By Mr. Gordon.

Ques. You have been connected with the Canal Company and have a knowledge of boats?
Ans. Yes.

Ques. How long will a dirt scow last and be good for anything?
Ans. In a general way from six to eight years. I have known none to be used longer than eight years.

Ques. Do not they become useless as fast or faster if not used than if used?
Ans. If a scow was sunk and not used it might last longer.

LLOYD LOWE.

THOMAS SHERIDAN recalled.

By Mr. Gordon.

Ques. Do you know when the Government dam was built at Harper's Ferry? Did you furnish lumber for the coping of it?
Ans. Yes, sir.

Ques. When was that?
Ans. I think it was in 1859 or 1860. I know it was before the war.

THOS. SHERIDAN.

WEDNESDAY, MARCH 23d, 1870.

The Committee met at 9½ o'clock pursuant to adjournment.
Present—Messrs. Henry, (Chairman,) Clarke and Sellman.
WM. THOMPSON, of R., sworn.

By Mr. Gordon.

Ques. Were you present on the packet boat last November, going down to Georgetown, when George W. Spates, Mr. Poe and myself had a conversation in the little state-room in regard to a bill and receipt of H. P. Tasker for $1200?
Ans. Yes, sir.

Ques. Do you recollect that paper (marked receipt of H. P. Tasker & Co. for $1200?)

Ans. I recollect there was such a paper presented on the boat, and that looks like the paper.

Ques. Did Mr. Spates say that that was the paper he filed with his abstract?

Ans. When I went to the door of the state-room, Mr. Spates, Mr. Gordon and Mr. Poe were inside. As I stood at the door, Mr. Gordon or Mr. Poe asked Mr. Spates if he paid that bill, and he said he did, and that was one of his vouchers. I did not take hold of the paper, but I saw the bill Mr. Poe had afterwards, and I am satisfied that is the paper. Mr. Poe asked him whom he got the bill from, and he said it was sent to him, and he went to Cumberland and paid it.

Cross-Examination by Mr. Schley.

Ques. You say you have no means of identifying that as the paper?

Ans. No, sir; I did not have the paper in my hand. And I did not stay at the door more than two or three seconds.

NEILSON POE sworn.

By Mr. Gordon.

Ques. Look at the paper now shown to you, (marked receipt of H. P. Tasker & Co. for $1,200,) and state whether that is the paper presented to Geo. W. Spates on the canal boat?

Ans. It is. I identify the paper.

Ques. State what he was asked about it and what he replied?

Ans. This paper and his abstract were presented to Mr. Spates, and he was asked if that was his voucher, and he stated that it was. He made no statement in regard to the paper, except to say that that was the paper which he had filed.

Mr. Gordon stated that he would rest his case here.

Mr. Schley presented the deposition of N. J. Berston, which was accepted by the Committee.

STATE OF MARYLAND, } Sct
Allegany County,

I hereby certify that I did, on the twenty-first day of March, in the year eighteen hundred and seventy, proceed to the dwelling house of N. J. Berston, in the city of Cumberland, and then and there, in the presence of J. M. Schley, attorney for Alfred Spates, Esq., in the matter now under investigation before the Senate Committee, appointed by virtue of an order passed by the Senate of Maryland, to investigate certain charges made by a committee of the Directors of the Chesapeake and Ohio Canal Board against said Spates, caused the said N. J. Berston to be brought before me, and did then and there administer an oath to the said N J Berston, according to law, to true answers make to the following interrogatories proposed to the witness, N. J. Berston, produced on the part of A. Spates, Esq.. I further certify that I did truly, faithfully, and without partiality to any or either of the parties in this case, take, write down, the depositions of the said N. J. Berston. I further certify that I caused the said N. J. Berston to subscribe his name to the depositions in my presence.

J. M. STRONG, J. P.

State of Maryland, Allegany County, } *To wit:*

I hereby certify that on the 21st day of March, 1870, I administered the following oath to Joseph M. Strong, a Justice of the Peace of the State of Maryland in and for Allegany County.

You, Joseph M. Strong, do solemnly and sincerely declare and affirm that you will truly, faithfully, and without partiality to any or either of the parties, in the case now pending before a Committee of Senators, appointed by virtue of an order of the Senate of Maryland, to inquire into certain charges preferred by a committee of the Directors of the Chesapeake and Ohio Canal Board against Alfred Spates, Esq, late President of the said Chesapeake and Ohio Canal Company, take and write down the depositions of N. J. Berston to the interrogatories which may hereafter be propounded to the said N. J. Berston.

Sworn to before me,

H. WHITE,
Justice of the Peace of the State of Maryland,
in and for Allegany County.

Interrogatories Proposed to N. J. Berston, a Witness Produced on the Part of A. Spates, Esq.

First—Where do you live?

Second—What is your occupation?

Third—How long have you been in the employment of the Chesapeake and Ohio Canal Company?

Fourth—Do you know how many ice breakers were built in Cumberland in the year eighteen hundred and sixty-seven?

Fifth—Do you know what Divisions of the Canal received those ice breakers?

Sixth—Did or did not the Canal Company's hands build all three?

Seventh—Did or did not country wagons deliver lumber from time to time for one of the ice breakers built in the Company's yard, and not paid for by the Canal Company?

Eighth—Do you or not know how many feet of lumber is in an ice breaker sixty feet long and three feet high on the sides?

Ninth—Do you or not know how many boats were built on the Cumberland Division in the fall of eighteen hundred and sixty-eight?

Tenth—Do you or not know how many feet of lumber are in a house boat?

Eleventh—Did or did not the Canal Company get from Tasker & Co. lumber in the fall of eighteen hundred and sixty-eight?

Twelfth—Do you or not know the cost of a house boat?

Thirteenth—Did or did you not get lumber and iron from Alfred Spates for the use of the Canal Company, to be repaid in lumber when called on by A. Spates?

Fourteenth—What was the lumber and iron gotten by you (independent of the iron gotten by R. M. Sprigg from the said Alfred Spates) worth?

Fifteenth—Did you or not settle with Alfred Spates by sending him two lots of lumber from J. J. Bruce, amounting to the sum of $644.94, in part payment of the $750?

Sixteenth—How was the balance of the $750 paid to Spates?

To the First Interrogatory the witness, N. J. Berston, answers and says:

"In Cumberland."

To the Second Interrogatory the witness answers and says:

"I am a carpenter."

To the Third Interrogatory the witness answers and says:

"About eight years."

To the Fourth Interrogatory the witness answers and says:

"There was three ice breakers built in Cumberland in the year 1867."

To the Fifth Interrogatory the witness answers and says:

"George W. Spates, Isaac R. Mans, and one remained on the Cumberland Division."

To the Sixth Interrogatory the witness answers and says:

"There was a dozen other hands besides the Company's hands employed in building them, and some I did not know."

N. J. BERSTON.

To the Seventh Interrogatory the witness answers and says:

"There was country wagons delivered lumber at the basin above, and floated down to the Company's yard; who bought it or paid for it, I do not know; it was not my business to inquire."

To the Eighth Interrogatory the witness answers and says:
"I should suppose that there is about fifteen thousand feet."

To the Ninth Interrogatory the witness answers and says:
"There were five boats built."

To the Tenth Interrogatory the witness answers and says:
"I suppose there is eighteen or twenty thousand feet."

To the Eleventh Interrogatory the witness answers and says:
"I ordered from Tasker & Co. lumber for house boat, ice-breaker and mud machine.

N. J. BERSTON.

To the Twelfth Interrogatory the witness answers and says:
"From eighteen hundred to two thousand dollars."

To the Thirteenth Interrogatory the witness answers and says:
"I did."

To the Fourteenth Interrogatory the witness answers and says:
"Seven hundred and fifty dollars."

To the Fifteenth Interrogatory the witness answers and says:
"I did."

To the Sixteenth Interrogatory the witness answers and says:
"The balance was paid by work on his carriage house."

N. J. BERSTON.

R. M. Sprigg recalled.

By Mr. Schley.

Ques. Were you in Cumberland yesterday morning?
Ans. Yes, sir.

Ques. Did you or not look at the switch at the back of Gephart's watch-house, and if so, state how many car loads of lumber you saw standing on it yesterday morning?
Ans. There were three car loads standing there, and there was room for one more, and ten feet to spare.

R. M. SPRIGG.

The case was then submitted to the Committee without argument.

REPORT

OF THE

Special Committee on Investigation

OF THE

HON. ALFRED SPATES.

Report Adopted April 1st, 1870.

REPORT.

The Special Committee appointed under the order of the Senate, passed on the 18th day of February, 1870, at the instance of the Senator from Allegany county, respectfully report:—

That they entered upon the discharge of the duty assigned them by the order referred to, at the earliest moment at their command, with the intention and desire to make their investigation as thorough and exhaustive as circumstances would permit. Believing that the charges contained in the report of the Committee on Accounts of the Chesapeake and Ohio Canal Company against the Senator from Allegany, constituted the chief motive for their appointment, and having no knowledge of any other matters connected with the administration of the affairs of that Company requiring special examination, they felt that it would be impossible for them, within any reasonable time, or with any degree of fairness, to fulfill the purpose of the Senate, unless they permitted the attendance and availed themselves of the aid of the parties personally interested in the result of their inquiries. Accordingly, J. H. Gordon, Esq., President of the Canal Company, and the Senator from Allegany, were both invited to be present at the sessions of the Committee, either in person or by counsel, to take such part as is usual in the conduct of cases. Mr. Gordon and Neilson Poe, Esq., under the invitation, attended in support of the charges contained in the report of the Committee on Accounts, and Col. Spates,

with Col. J. M. Schley as his counsel, for the defence.—
Orders were promptly given for the summoning of all witnesses desired on either side, and the Sergeant-at-Arms succeeded in every case in serving the process. The witnesses all attended with commendable punctuality, with the exception of N. J. Berston, of Cumberland, whose delicate health rendered it unsafe for him to leave home. His testimony was taken, however, on interrogatories before a Justice of the Peace, by order of the Committee, and will be found in its proper place. When ready to proceed, it was determined to take up the charges contained in the report of the Committee on Accounts in regular order, and as far as practicable, to hear, first, all the evidence to maintain them, then to hear the evidence for the defence, and afterwards to close with the rebutting evidence. At this late period of the session, when the members of the Committee are pressed with other urgent and important duties, it will not be possible for them to make an elaborate exposition of the points in the testimony. All that they can do is to present a brief synopsis of material facts, sufficient to justify the conclusions at which they have unanimously and without difficulty arrived, after an attentive hearing of all the evidence as it was delivered, and a careful examination of it since. It is due to the Senator whose character was involved that the result of this investigation should not be longer withheld, and the Committee therefore submit this report, with all the testimony and proceedings appended, so that the Senate and the public can determine upon the correctness of the conclusion adopted. As preliminary, however, to a review of the charges and the evidence relating to them, it is proper to remark, that the affidavits and other information on which these charges were made, and which it is presumed were sufficient to make out a *prima facie* case, not being legally admissible, were not submitted to the Committee; but that during the whole progress of the investigation the Committee were forcibly impressed with the importance of that time-honored and essential test of truth (cross-examination,)

and with the danger of relying too implicitly on the *ex parte* affidavits of voluntary witnesses, especially in a time of political rancor and interested partizanship. It is true, that notice of the intended investigation was given to Col. Spates by the Committee on Accounts, and he has, no doubt, been subjected to injurious imputations and suspicions, which he might have avoided by his appearance before them, but his letter to Mr. Poe, and the statement of Col. Schley, to be found in the testimy, show that he acted under advice, and with a just sense of propriety under all the circumstances.

First.—The first charge made in the report of the Committee on Accounts is, in substance, a charge of forging a receipt for $800, for "building, ironing, painting and finishing one ice breaker for use of Georgetown Division," signed "Thomas Sheridan," and sent by Col. Spates to Isaac R. Maus, Superintendent of Georgetown Division, as a voucher to be used by him. To support this charge, it was proved that Maus, about December, 1867, sent to Col. Spates $800 to pay for an ice breaker; that Col. Spates sent to him a receipt for that amount signed "Thomas Sheridan;" that Maus received the ice breaker, filed the receipt in the Canal office, and claimed credit for its amount in his abstract of expenditures; that the abstract was examined by the Committee on Accounts of the Canal Company, approved and allowed; that one Thomas Sheridan, a boat-builder and manager for Henry Thomas Weld, and a resident of Cumberland for many years, did not build any ice breaker in 1867 for the Canal Company, and that he did not receive $800 from the Company or anybody acting for it, and that he did not execute the receipt for that amount offered in evidence. It was also proved by several witnesses, that although it was probable they would have known if there had been any other Thomas Sheridan than the one above named building a boat in Cumberland, yet they never knew any other of that name, except a son of the said Thomas, who was but a boy, and not a boat-builder. For the defence, it was proved, beyond doubt, that there were three ice breakers built for the

Canal Company in 1867; that there was nothing to show that more than two of them had ever been paid for, except the receipt and abstract referred to above; that R. M. Sprigg, Superintendent of the Cumberland Division, employed another Thomas Sheridan, a stranger and mere sojourner in Cumberland, to build one of the three ice breakers; that this Thomas Sheridan had left Cumberland and gone West, and Sprigg had since made diligent inquiry for him, but could not discover his whereabouts. There was no evidence as to the handwriting of the receipt. By the testimony—of which the foregoing is but a brief summary—the committee were satisfied that the receipt in question represented a genuine transaction, and that there was no foundation upon which the first charge could rest..

Second and *Third.*—These charges are so connected in the testimony, and in the transactions upon which they are based, that they will be considered together. The second asserts that Col. Spates undertook to expend $1,000 in Cumberland for John Shay, Superintendent of Antietam Division, for a scow, lumber, and paddle-frames, and that he obtained from J. J. Bruce a receipt for $652.60, when $400 of that amount had already been paid by Mr. Sprigg, which receipt was sent to and innocently used by Mr. Shay as a voucher, and that the result was a clear gain to Col. Spates and loss to the Company of $400. The third is of the same character, except that it alleges that Col. Spates obtained from J. J. Bruce for Isaac R. Maus, Superintendent of the Georgetown Division, a duplicate receipt, to be used by him as a voucher for $400, when no money was paid for it by Col. Spates, and the lumber which it represented had already been paid for by Mr. Sprigg.

The maintenance of these charges depends entirely upon the testimony of Dr. J. J. Bruce. It does not appear at what time he volunteered to give to the Committee on Accounts of the Canal Company the affidavit on which their report relies, whether before or after the election in November last; nor is this very material. Dr. Bruce was, or had been, at that election, a candidate for the State Senate in opposition to Col. Spates. Great bitterness of feeling manifested itself throughout the contest, as the cards to be found among the testimony too plainly show. And this Committee feel constrained to say that, under the circumstances, they think Dr. Bruce committed a grave error in making such an affidavit when he was not acting under the compulsion of the law. They are also of opinion, if his recollection be correct, that he cannot be commended for the ready facility with which, according to his statements, he gave duplicate receipts without stating upon their face that they were such, for accounts which had already been paid, wholly or in part. The fact that Col. Spates was, at that time, President of the Chesapeake and Ohio Canal Company, could not vary the nature of such complaisance. Dr. Bruce, in his testimony, states positively that $400 of the amount embraced in the account and receipt for $652.60, had already been paid by Mr. Sprigg, and that the account and receipt for $400 was only a duplicate, the whole amount having been paid by Mr. Sprigg; and that these accounts and receipts, with the exception of $252.60, paid by Col. Spates, were both embraced in an account and receipt for $1,257.10, for lumber previously paid for by Mr. Sprigg. All these receipts are written at the bottom of accounts for lumber, containing numerous items, and the accounts and receipts are all acknowledged to be in the handwriting of Dr. Bruce.

R. M. Sprigg, for the defense, testified positively that he went with Col. Spates to Dr. Bruce's and *saw him* pay Dr. Bruce $1,052.60, the exact sum of the two receipts in question, and relates various circumstances connected with the transaction, calculated to impress the facts upon his memory. His testimony is affirmative; Dr. Bruce's rather negative in its character. On a careful comparison of the items in the two accounts, which were receipted and delivered to Col. Spates, with the items in the account for $1,257.10, in which it is alleged they are embraced, the committee have not been able to recognize any two items as corresponding. Dr.

Bruce, however, on his cross-examination, pointed out one item in one of them, which he said was the same with another item in another, although of a different date and called by a different name. There was other testimony on both sides in reference to these charges, which the committee regard as less material, and, therefore, do not notice. It will all be found with the record submitted with this Report, and to that they must refer. After hearing and examining it all, they decide, without hesitation, that the Second and Third Charges are not sustained.

Fourth.—The Fourth Charge is in substance that Col. Spates furnished George W. Spates, Superintendent of the Seneca Division, with the means of embezzling the funds of the Canal Company by sending him two receipts for lumber, purporting to have been given by H. P. Tasker & Co., when in point of fact they never gave any such receipts, nor sold the lumber which they represented to Geo. W. Spates, or to the Canal Company, or to any one on behalf of either. The charge also contains an inuendo that Col. Spates received the money and appropriated it to his own use. The testimony applicable to this charge is quite voluminous, and it is not possible for the Committee, without extending their report to an unreasonable length, to give anything like an adequate summary of it. On one side, evidence was offered to prove that the receipts referred to were not given by H. P. Tasker & Co.; that they were copied from similar ones, not in the handwriting of Col. Spates, by the Deputy Clerk of the Circuit Court for Allegany county, at the request of Col. Spates, on two bill-heads of the firm, furnished at his request, for the purpose of separating the items of account; that the lumber for which they were given was never furnished by H. P. Tasker & Co., as alleged, and the receipts were identified by Mr. Fawcett, Clerk and Treasurer of the Canal Company, as the same filed in the Canal office by George W. Spates, as vouchers, by memorandum on them in the handwriting of Mr. Peck, a clerk in the Canal office. On the other side, evidence was introduced to prove that H. P. Tasker retired from the firm of H. P. Tasker & Co. on account of some dissatisfaction in the firm; that at the time of his retiring there appeared to be a deficiency in the lumber on hand of some thirty or forty thousand feet, which the Committee think was not satisfactorily explained; that some three and a-half car loads of lumber were about that time furnished to the Canal Company by H. P. Tasker & Co.—that Geo. W. Spates received the ice-breaker, in the construction of which it is alleged the lumber was used. By Geo. W. Spates, that he did not know H. P. Tasker, or any of his clerks, but paid the money to some one acting for the firm, with whom he was not acquainted, and took receipts for the same; that the receipts offered in evidence are not the same which he filed in Canal Office. By Mr. Peck, that the numbering by which Mr. Fawcett identified the receipts was not in his handwriting, and that Geo. W. Spates's account, in which these receipts are embraced, was examined and approved by the proper authorities of the Canal Company, while the transactions were recent. The originals from which these receipts were copied were not produced, nor was any explanation given of what had become of them, although notice to produce them was given by the counsel for the defense. The testimony was conflicting on various points, but the Committee think the preponderance of the whole was largely in favor of the defense, and they have no hesitancy in entirely acquitting Col. Spates of this charge.

Fifth.—The purport of the 5th charge is, that Spates undertook to procure for Mr. Thomas, Superintendent of Monocacy Division, a mud machine and scow, and to disburse the money for that purpose, amounting to some $1,600.00, and that among the vouchers for this expenditure to be filed by Mr. Thomas, as an honest man, there were two, the fraudulent character of which was satisfactorily established, *one* a bill and a receipt for $108.25, apparently executed by John Snyder & Co., in the handwriting of the same person, who copied the Tasker bills; and the *other*, a bill and receipt apparently executed by Henry Snyder for $350.00; that these vouchers were spurious, or in other words forgeries, and that Col. Spates pocketed the whole amount for which they were given, with the exception of $25.00. This charge was abandoned very properly by Messrs. Gordon and Poe, so far as the first mentioned receipt is concerned, John Snyder testifying that said receipt was genuine, and that he had testified falsely before the Committee on Accounts of the Canal Company. His explanation will appear by reference to the testimony.

In regard to the $350.00 receipt, Mr. Thomas testified that he had applied to the Company for a scow and mud machine in the spring of 1869, that Col. Spates purchased the scow and sent him the receipt for $350.00, which he returned to the Canal Office, and that the scow was worth $350.00 and cheap at that. Henry Snyder stated that he had never built a scow for the Canal Company or sold one to them; that he did not write English; never saw the receipt for $350.00 until it was shown to him by Mr. Gordon in the boat yard; that he had lived seventeen years in Cumberland; was a boat-builder, and did not know any other boat-builder of that name in Cumberland. Jas. J. McHenry testified that he was a lawyer in Cumberland; that he made out the $350.00 receipt for Col. Spates, for whom he frequently did writing; that the receipt was not signed in his presence; that there was a stranger with Col. Spates, whom he said he wanted to pay, &c. For the defense evidence was introduced to prove the order of the Canal Board, authorizing Col. Spates, President and Superintendent, to procure a scow and mud machine for Monocacy Division. By A. K. Stake, at that time one of the Directors of the Canal Company, it was proved that he was consulted by Col. Spates as to the purchase of a scow that had been used at Harper's Ferry, and was offered to him by a man named Snyder. In this instance, as in the case of charge first, the receipt evidently represents a real transaction. The scow, a second hand one, was evidently furnished, and was cheap at the price charged for it. No evidence of any payment for it was introduced except the receipt for $350.00, and the Committee are of opinion that the charge has been completely refuted.

Sixth.—This charge relates to the expenditure of $10,000 furnished by the Canal Company to be applied in payment for the condemnation of certain lands which the Company wished to acquire, and alleges that a successful and deliberate attempt at embezzlement in accounting for the expenditure of this money was made by Col. Spates, by returning as one of his vouchers an altered record of the condemnation of certain lands of Henry Thomas Weld and wife, which had been previously paid for in September, 1866, and that by this means the sum of $739.00 was left in the possession of Col. Spates from March, 1868, to September, 1869, when his attention being drawn to it, he promptly refunded the money.

To support this charge, the order of the Canal Board, passed March 11th, 1868, placing $10.000 in the hands of Col. Spates to pay for certain lands to be condemned for the use of the Company, was offered in evidence, also a correct copy of the record of condemnation of the Weld lands, and an altered or incorrect copy of the same. Mr. Fawcett also produced certain vouchers, and testified that they were filed by Col. Spates January 7th, 1869, of which one was the altered copy of the record mentioned above; that the amount of the vouchers exceeded the amount appropriated by $850.79, which last mentioned amount was subsequently paid to Col. Spates, and that he was clerk of the Company when the Weld record was filed, and Col. Spates received the allowance. Percival Rowland testified, that he was deputy clerk of the Circuit Court for Allegany county, and made out correctly the copy of the record, which had been altered, and pointed out in various places where he was satisfied the word "six" and the figure "six" had been changed to word "eight" and the figure "eight," so as to change the date of the record from the year 1866 to 1868, and that the word "late" had been prefixed to the word

13

Sheriff. There is no evidence to show at what time, or by whom the alterations were made, nor did Mr. Rowland know by whom the copy was ordered, to whom it was delivered, or at what time he made it out.

The defense offered in evidence a letter of Mr. Gordon, as President of the Canal Company, to Col. Spates, dated September 14th, 1869, in which he calls his attention to the Weld case, and states that he had claimed and received a credit for that amount of money from the Canal Company, which he did not pay and had no right to, and requests an explanation of the matter at once.

Mr. Gordon, being called as a witness by the defense, testified that at the time his letter was written, he was not on speaking terms with Col. Spates; that after the receipt of his letter, Col. Spates had an interview with him as he was passing the railroad, in which Col. Spates stated that he had the money in bank, and would place it to the credit of the Canal Company, and said something about an explanation, which witness told him had better be made in writing; that Col. Spates replied that would not be necessary, as he would place the money to the credit of the Canal Company; thinks that Col. Spates told him he knew nothing about the thing; that he did state that if the receipt was dated in 1868 it was a mistake; that it did not take place in his administration, but in that of Snively; that he had nothing to do with the thing, but would go to the bank and investigate it and come to witness' office and show him the whole transaction; that it had all been done by Roman; that Col. Spates came to his office on the same day and exhibited some checks, how many not known, and witness looked over them and saw they were in Mr. Roman's handwriting; that Col. Spates stated further, that Mr. Roman had charge of the whole thing, and had drawn the checks upon the fund; that this was a mistake; that he knew nothing about it, and had transferred the amount to the Company; recollected distinctly the receipts now shown to him; did not know how many, and thought they were in Mr. Roman's handwriting;

that he did not receive the explanation as satisfactory at the time in regard to the $739, because Col. Spates had no receipt for that; then it was understood between them it was settled; that settled that amount of it, and that witness a week afterwards published his circular, for the reason that Col. Spates had been making statements in regard to him.

The defense also offered in evidence the certificate of deposit for $739.00 dated September 16th, 1869. In the charge itself, it is stated, that by some oversight, the counsel of the Canal Company had omitted to enter a satisfaction of the Weld judgment on the docket of the Court until the 9th of December, 1868. After due consideration of all the testimony, this Committee agree with the Committee on Accounts of the Canal Company, that there is no evidence to show by whom the alteration and falsification of the record in the Weld case, or rather of the copy of it offered in evidence, was made, and they are not aware of any rule of law or principle of justice, which would justify them in presuming that they were the work of Col. Spates. They can readily understand how such a paper might be inadvertently and innocently used, and how easily a mistake might be made in a series of transactions such as these. The supposition that any one of ordinary intelligence would attempt, with a fraudulent purpose, to falsify or alter the copy of a public record when the record itself, open to the inspection of all, affords a sure means of detection, is almost too improbable to be for one moment entertained. In case of a mistake, all that an honest man can do, is to correct it when his attention is called to it, and to make up any loss to others which it may have occasioned. The Canal Company, in this instance, was settled with, promptly and in full, and it is strange that their Committee on Accounts should have thought it within their duty to call attention to a transaction which they knew had been finally settled before their investigation commenced, and when the individual to be affected by it was no longer an officer of the Company. In the opinion of the Committee, the charge is not established by the proof, and they dismiss it without farther comment.

Seventh.—The seventh charge is, that Col. Spates, as President of the Canal Company, misapplied its funds against the remonstrance of Mr. Roman, the counsel of the Company, by the part payment of a judgment founded on scrip, which was deferred to the liens of the State and the bondholders, and while there were judgments of the same character, amounting to more than $100,000, and that this was a deliberate perversion of the funds of the Company, which cannot be too severely censured.

This charge, when understood, will be found trivial in itself, although it is alluded to also in the preceding charge. The witness to maintain it was Patrick Murray, an aged man, in indigent circumstances, who had lost an arm in the service of the Company, and held a claim against it for more than twelve hundred dollars, for work done by him, as a laborer on the Canal between the years 1837 and 1842. Being then out of work, he applied to Col. Spates, President of the Company, to get the money owing to him, two or three times. At first he promised to do so, but the last time witness thought he was a little cool.

He then applied to Mr. Roman and left the papers with him; he promised to get judgment for him, and did. Afterwards he had an interview with Col. Spates and Mr. Roman together, in Mr. Roman's office, and was paid $324.00 in part of his judgment. The receipt, which he signed, states that the money was received from Col. Spates, but the body of the receipt is in the handwriting of Mr. Roman, and the check with which it was paid is filled up in Mr. Roman's handwriting, and signed by him, "Alfred Spates, per J. Philip Roman, Attorney for Chesapeake and Ohio Canal Company." There was no consideration of any kind given or promised for this small payment, and if in making it a technical error was committed, it was one to which we are all liable, who are subject to the feelings of sympathy and compassion. The Committee do not feel called upon to say more in reference to this charge; it is disposed of by the testimony.

Eighth.—It is alleged in the eighth charge that an arrangement was made, to which the Canal Company was a party, for the removal of boats and wrecks from the basin at Cumberland, and that in carrying out this purpose Col. Spates received over and above the actual cost of this work the sum of $540.00, which he retained in his hands and has never accounted for.

The Committee do not deem it necessary to give any statement of the evidence applicable to this charge. The payment to the parties entitled of the $540.00 is clearly proved, and the whole matter fully explained by the witnesses, Willison, Sprigg and Humbird. The charge is disproved beyond all question.

Ninth.—The ninth and last charge asserts that Col. Spates purchased from J. J. Bruce, on his account, lumber to the value of $644.90, which he caused to be charged to, and paid for by the Canal Company, and for which he has never accounted.

There is no question that Col. Spates got the lumber and that it was charged to the Company, as alleged, and there can be no more question that the evidence of Sprigg, and the affidavit of Berston, show that they obtained from Colonel Spates, iron and lumber for the Canal Company to an equal or greater amount, and that the whole matter was settled by a fair exchange.

The Committee having thus disposed of all the charges set forth in the report of the Committee on Accounts, are not aware of any other matter or thing within the scope of the order appointing them, which demands investigation by them. This report, necessarily brief and imperfect, owing to the distractions of other important duties acquiring attention before the close of the session, does not profess to give more than a fair outline of the more material portions of the charges, proceedings and testimony, the record of which is submitted herewith, as an essential appendage to this report. An examination of this record will show that no reference has ever been made to some portions of the testimony, which throw various degrees of light upon the subject matter of inquiry, but which relate chiefly to collateral, though legitimate phases of the principal issues. They think it will also appear, that the investigation was carried through with impartiality and thoroughness, and with a determination on their part that it should not prove a sham. Of this, however, others are to judge. While the Committee are glad to be relieved of the labor incident to the duty which they have endeavored to fulfill, they may, in conclusion, be allowed to say, that they will be more than satisfied, if there should be a general concurrence of impartial and candid men, as they confidently believe there will be, in all that they have said in vindication of the integrity and honor of the Senator, whose character was involved.

        DAN'L M. HENRY,
            Chairman.
        JAS. C. CLARKE,
        WM. O. SELLMAN,
            Committee.

www.ingramcontent.com/pod-product-compliance
Lightning Source LLC
Chambersburg PA
CBHW020840160426

43192CB00007B/726